In the Driver's Seat

The Intelligent Road to Your Ultimate Retirement

Kurt T. Fillmore
Certified Financial Fiduciary®
Wealth Trac Financial

Copyright © 2023 by Kurt Fillmore.

All rights reserved. No part of this publication may be reproduced, distributed, or transmitted in any form or by any means, including photocopying, recording, or other electronic or mechanical methods, without the prior written permission of the publisher, except in the case of brief quotations embodied in critical reviews and certain other noncommercial uses permitted by copyright law. For permission requests, write to the publisher at the address below. These materials are provided to you by Kurt Fillmore for informational purposes only and Kurt Fillmore expressly disclaims any and all liability arising out of or relating to your use of same. The provision of these materials does not constitute legal or investment advice and does not establish an attorney-client relationship between you and Kurt Fillmore. No tax advice is contained in these materials. You are solely responsible for ensuring the accuracy and completeness of all materials as well as the compliance, validity, and enforceability of all materials under any applicable law. The advice and strategies found within may not be suitable for every situation. You are expressly advised to consult with a qualified attorney or other professional in making any such determination and to determine your legal or financial needs. No warranty of any kind, implied, expressed, or statutory, including but not limited to the warranties of title and non-infringement of third-party rights, is given with respect to this publication.

Kurt Fillmore/Wealth Trac Financial LLC
30777 Telegraph Road
Franklin, MI 48025
wealthtracfinancial.com

Book layout ©2023 Advisors Excel, LLC

In the Driver's Seat/Kurt Fillmore — 1st edition

ISBN 9798373174718

Kurt Fillmore is a fiduciary who is registered as an Investment Advisor Representative. He is a licensed insurance agent in many states across the USA and is a notary public in the state of Michigan. Wealth Trac Financial is an independent financial services firm helping individuals, families, and businesses create investment and retirement solutions using a variety of investment and insurance strategies to custom suit their needs and objectives.

Investment advisory services offered through CoreCap Advisors, LLC. Wealth Trac and CoreCap are separate and unaffiliated entities.

The contents of this book are provided for informational purposes only and are not intended to serve as the basis for any financial decisions. Any tax, legal, or estate planning information is general in nature. It should not be construed as legal or tax advice. Always consult an attorney or tax professional regarding the applicability of this information to your unique situation.

Information presented is believed to be factual and up-to-date, but we do not guarantee its accuracy, and it should not be regarded as a complete analysis of the subjects discussed. All expressions of opinion are those of the author as of the date of publication and are subject to change. Content should not be construed as personalized investment advice nor should it be interpreted as an offer to buy or sell any securities mentioned. A financial advisor should be consulted before implementing any of the strategies presented.

In order to protect the privacy of any clients mentioned herewithin, all details relating to their identity have been concealed or changed to the point that any resemblance to persons living or dead is strictly coincidental.

Retirement is not the end of the road.
It is the beginning of the open highway.

~ Unknown

This book is dedicated to all the financial advisors out there craving confirmation that there is a
better way of doing things,
and to their clients, my clients, and my future clients
who deserve nothing less.

Table of Contents

FINDING MY PURPOSE 1

CHOOSING A FINANCIAL ADVISOR 13
    WHY WAIT? 13
    DIFFERENTIATING BETWEEN ADVISORS 17
    CHECK THE ADVISOR'S DISCLOSURES & EXPERIENCE 19
    WHAT TO LOOK FOR IN AN ADVISOR 21
    FEE MODELS 22
    COMMUNICATIONS WITH AN ADVISOR 25
    FEELING COMFORTABLE AND CONFIDENT ABOUT RETIREMENT 27
    TAX PLANNING FOR RETIREMENT 28
    RED FLAGS TO LOOK OUT FOR 29

IT'S NOT WHAT YOU MAKE, IT'S WHAT YOU KEEP 33
    MONEY MINDFULNESS 33
    EVALUATING YOUR LIFESTYLE 35
    MAKING CONSCIOUS CHOICES ABOUT MONEY 37
    THE PROBLEM WITH BUDGETING 39
    BROADENING YOUR PERSPECTIVES 40
    CONSIDERING LUXURIES & EMOTIONAL INVESTMENTS 43
    THE BIG PICTURE 46

RETIREMENT IS ABOUT MORE THAN MONEY 49
    DO I WANT TO STOP WORKING? 49
    RETIREMENT LIFESTYLE 51
    TIME IN RETIREMENT 53
    UNRETIRING 54
    AGE AND THE WORKPLACE 54
    SLOW RETIREMENT AND RETIRING EARLIER 56
    LIFESTYLE, SPENDING, AND TAXES 58
    THE PHASES OF RETIREMENT 61

YOU'RE THE ONE ON THE HOOK 63
    THE NEW RETIREMENT 64
    PENSIONS 66

PENSION REPLACEMENT	72
THE COLLEGE DISTRACTION	72

SOCIAL SECURITY 79

SOCIAL SECURITY BASICS	80
TO DEFER OR NOT TO DEFER	81
IT'S NOT THAT SIMPLE	83
THE LONGEVITY QUESTION	86

YOU'LL NEED MORE, NOT LESS 89

HEALTHCARE	90
MEDICARE	93
LONG-TERM CARE	99
LET YOURSELF SPEND...	102
...BUT DON'T OVERSPEND PREMATURELY	103

WOMEN AND RETIREMENT 111

HAVING THE TOUGH FINANCIAL CONVERSATIONS	113
INVITING BOTH SPOUSES TO THE TABLE	115
MAKING FINANCIAL DECISIONS TOGETHER	116
KEEPING TRACK OF FINANCES	119
PROVIDING CARE	119
FUNDING YOUR OWN RETIREMENT AND SAVING MONEY	121

YOU CAN'T TAKE IT WITH YOU 123

ESTABLISHING AN ESTATE PLAN	123
MAKE A DIGITAL COPY	125
THE ONE HUNDRED YEAR PLAN	125
HELPING SURVIVORS	126
PUTTING AFFAIRS IN ORDER	127
THE NEXT GENERATION	129

ACKNOWLEDGMENTS 131

ABOUT THE AUTHOR 133

CHAPTER 1
Finding My Purpose

November 23rd, 1996. A quintessential midwestern Fall day. Red and yellow leaves crunching beneath footsteps. Brisk breezes tickling noses. The sweet smell of plants and flowers resting for the season. Clear and sunny skies reminding of a summer now past. It was a perfect day for a football game in Ann Arbor, Michigan.

I was a nineteen-year-old sophomore. I awoke that day like many other University of Michigan students, with nervous anticipation. I walked to the gym early and nodded at fellow students crossing my path along the way, locking eyes briefly with an unspoken understanding that today was *the big day*. The gym was quiet, the tension palpable, minds focused on finishing their workout before Ann Arbor unofficially shut down for the day. The town's most anticipated event of the year was happening that afternoon.

I walked back in silence to my fraternity house. My head down, hands in pockets. Around me, the town was starting to wake up. Like a rooster's crow, the deep bass of music permeated the air, alerting fast-asleep students that this was not a typical Saturday. Tents and canopies stabbed into dirt, becoming temporary shelters. Grilled hot dogs and burgers wafted their scents through cracked-open windows. The big day was upon us.

Despite it being an away game, the crowds grew bigger and bigger in the Ann Arbor streets. Lawns swelled with waves of maize and blue as people crowded together with united purpose. The tension mounted higher and higher as the countdown toward noon marched forward. This was a game unlike any other game of the season. Even those who don't normally follow football, they paid attention today.

The Michigan Wolverines football team traveled down to Columbus, Ohio, to continue the tradition of playing the final regular season game against the Ohio State Buckeyes. The matchup is known as the biggest rivalry in sports, and anyone who supports either team would agree. We were the defending champions after pulling off an upset victory on home turf the previous year. This year's rematch on OSU soil was going to be their revenge.

Leading up to the final game of the regular season, the Buckeyes were undefeated 11-0, just as they were the previous year. They were ranked number-two among all college football teams. Michigan was ranked number twenty-one with a 7-3 record. Ohio had homefield advantage this year. They were favored to win by a huge seventeen-point margin.

While other people tailgated and went to bars and restaurants to watch the game, I preferred to avoid distractions. I stayed back at my fraternity house with a small group of guys, sitting together in stillness leading up to kickoff. I sat and waited, postured tensely on the edge of the sofa, focused intently on the TV.

The ball snapped. The game was officially in motion.

Ohio State proved dominant early on. Michigan was unable to make plays or get points on the board. Then, just before halftime, Michigan's starting quarterback injured his elbow and was out for the game. Going into halftime, they were being shut out 0-9.

Second-string quarterback, Brian Griese, took the field carrying the weight of the world on his shoulders. Despite being the previous year's starting quarterback, Griese had only thrown ten passes all season. This was his moment to shine, to take center stage and prove his worth as a quarterback to the world. He would either rise to the occasion or crumble beneath the pressure. He finished the first half unimpressive.

Needless to say, it was not looking good for the Wolverines.

The second half began. Griese handed off the ball to a receiver. The ball moved forward for a two-yard gain before being stopped abruptly by a swarm of red and white. Michigan could not get momentum.

And then it happened; the momentum shifted. On the second play of the second half, Griese threw a slant pass for a sixty-nine yard touchdown! Michigan fans erupted in cheer. After the successful extra point, the score was a tight 7-9. Hope was still alive.

The ball passed back and forth from one possession to the next, taking turns across the field like a game of ping-pong. After a successful long field goal attempt, the third quarter drew to a close with Michigan taking the lead 10-9.

Another field goal completion put Michigan up 13-9 with 01:19 left on the clock. We cheered and held our breath simultaneously. The Buckeyes had one last possession to try for the win.

Michigan kicked off. OSU caught the ball way down at their two-yard line. One first down followed by three incomplete passes left the Buckeyes at third down and twenty-one. It seemed Michigan's victory was within reach.

But then the Buckeyes threw a twenty-five yard pass for the first down. And then an eighteen-yard pass for another first down. I could barely watch, my stomach in knots, as OSU advanced down the field.

Then the tide turned again. Michigan's defense responded with a series of impressive stops. 0:04 seconds on the clock and the score was still 13-9. The Buckeyes had one last chance to reclaim the win.

Just as the final play was about to snap, OSU called a timeout. The wait was excruciating as they attempted to coordinate one last miracle move. My hands on my hips, I paced back and forth until the players ran back on the field and took their positions. The ball snapped. The OSU quarterback looked downfield and threw the Hail Mary. The crowd held its breath and went silent. The ball lingered in the air for an eternity. When the ball descended, it landed directly in the hands of a Wolverine. A Michigan interception with 0:00 left on the clock! Against all odds, we had won!

My fraternity brothers and I jumped up and down, screaming in joy at the excitement and drama that had just ensued. This game would go down in history as one of the most exciting, thrilling games in all of college football. We understood the significance of that game in that moment.

Outside the fraternity walls, we could hear cars honking and music playing. The town was celebrating. Now that the game was over, I felt a wave of relief and wanted to join in the celebration. I went back to my dorm room to grab my coat.

As I left the living room, the faint sound of a phone ringing in the distance caught my attention. The repetitive ringing grew louder and louder as I approached my hallway. The phone continued to ring, over and over, with unrelenting desperation, until I opened my door and picked up the receiver.

"Hello?" I answered. It was my brother's voice, but his tone was somber. I immediately knew something was wrong.

What followed are three words I will never forget.

"Dad died today."

What happened after that was a blur. The quick shift in mood from euphoria to grief was shocking to my system. I remember hanging up the phone and going into the hallway. I gripped my hair with both hands on my head, elbows outreached, walking and pacing and trying to process the news. A friend saw me and asked if I was okay. I told him, "I just found out my dad died." He didn't know how to react, and frankly, I didn't either. This was a new, unfamiliar reality.

Dad was not old. He was generally healthy. He led an active life. As a teenager, I was not prepared to lose my father. The news of his death struck me as a complete surprise.

Even though Dad underwent heart bypass surgery about six-months prior, he had recovered quickly, resumed normal activities, and was doing well for many months. Then Dad went in for routine hernia surgery and never healed. His body was not ready to endure a surgery, however minor or routine. A week after that hernia procedure, my brother had to share life's heaviest words with his little brother over the phone.

The following weeks and months were a blur of activity and emotion as we arranged Dad's funeral and tried to make sense of what he left behind. My parents were divorced, so my brother and I assumed responsibility for handling Dad's affairs. We had to figure out how to handle his house, his possessions, and his finances. I was completely unprepared and in over my head.

I didn't know it then, but this was the start of my very long journey to a real financial education.

Even though he made a relatively modest income as a teacher, Dad always saved toward retirement. He had saved up about $240,000 in his IRA. My brother and I inherited his house and equally split the IRA.

As a busy college student, I left my $120,000 portion under the direction of Dad's financial advisor, who promptly invested it in mutual funds that were turning impressive profits during the go-go mid-1990s era of booming tech stocks. It looked really great at the time, but so did all kinds of doomed investments, from grocery delivery services like Webvan and HomeGrocer that would bring a single loaf of bread to your home, to the iSmell gizmo that plugged into your computer's USB port to generate smells. The tech boom busted in just a few years and, combined with some mistakes and outright conflicts of interest on the part of the financial advisor, that money was just a fraction of its original value by the end of 2001.

In college, I had been uncertain about the exact career path I wanted to take, but I knew I was interested in a business degree. Considering that the University of Michigan had the number-one ranked undergraduate business school in the country at the time, I figured getting accepted into this exclusive program would provide a good start toward a successful career. I worked very hard my first two years in Ann Arbor. It paid off when I was accepted into the ultra-competitive business school that spans both junior and senior years.

During those two years, I was exposed to all sides of the business world. I was always drawn toward Finance because it came naturally to me. Using numbers to solve problems has always been something that I very much enjoy, and I respect how important accuracy is in achieving optimum results.

During this time, it became clear that I needed to focus on the career path that would suit me best. Dozens of large, well-respected corporations recruit heavily from the U-M business school, so I was given the opportunity to interview with numerous firms for all sorts of positions. One of the most prestigious fields to enter at the time was business consulting. This appealed to me because of the variety it offered. Working at many different corporations across all types of industries would keep things interesting. The fact that each project would always be a new challenge was attractive. I've also always loved traveling, so the opportunity to see different parts of the county was an added bonus for me.

In 1999, I graduated with my business degree and started my career in business consulting. I spent a lot of time in Cleveland during the workweek doing supply chain management for companies like Royal Appliance (Dirt Devil) and American Greetings (greeting cards). While on the road, I was making a good living and was able to save a large portion of my income. Many of my expenses like lodging and fuel were covered by my employer while on assignment, and the Royal Oak house back home that my brother and I inherited from Dad was paid off. I've always been a saver at heart, so I socked away most of my income and started to build my financial foundation.

The huge financial loss I experienced with Dad's money was disappointing but not devastating. I was young and a good saver, so I could walk away from that loss without impacting my future too much. It would have been a completely different situation had that money been my life savings and I was nearing or already in retirement. I thought about that advisor who irresponsibly invested my dad's financial legacy, and how his average client in the 55+ age bracket would have felt that loss very differently.

I continued working on the road as a consultant and saving up for a couple of years. I was grateful to have time on my side to build up my nest egg, especially after losing most of Dad's inheritance. During this time, I often reflected back on how lucky I was to have learned this important financial lesson young, and I felt outraged that other families would not have the same opportunity to rebuild their losses.

Right around the same time, another major life event occurred that shifted my professional life forever. Although I was hundreds of miles away from the World Trade Center when the terrorist attacks happened on September 11th, 2001, like every American, I was shocked, outraged, and saddened. But unlike most Americans, I had a personal connection to 9/11 that impacted me and my life outlook forever.

The Cantor Fitzgerald investment bank is a dream job for many business graduates, including one of my eight fraternity pledge brothers, Todd. In 2001, Cantor Fitzgerald handled one-quarter of all transactions in the multi-trillion-dollar treasury security market, operating across the globe with 1,600 employees in more than thirty offices. Their New York City office was located on the 101st through 105th floors of One World Trade Center in Lower Manhattan. At 8:46

a.m. on 9/11/2001, a highjacked jetliner slammed into the 93rd through 99th floors, just a few floors beneath Cantor Fitzgerald. The destruction killed over 68 percent of Cantor Fitzgerald's workforce—more loss of life that day than any other World Trade Center tenant, more than the New York City Police Department, more than the Port Authority of New York, more than the New Jersey Police Department, even more than the New York City Fire Department. Of 960 New York employees at Cantor Fitzgerald, 658 were suddenly gone.

That list included Todd.

At 5-feet, 5-inches tall, Todd was an energetic guy who lit up a room. It had been Todd's dream to work for a Wall Street firm. He applied to the business school at U-M a few times and always fell just short, but he still pushed to pursue his Wall Street dreams. He graduated with a degree in psychology, moved back to his home state of New Jersey, and landed a job at the prestigious Cantor Fitzgerald firm as a foreign currency options trader.

Always the go-getter, Todd arrived early at work that fateful day. Most people in the building showed up at 9 o'clock, but like most Cantor Fitzgerald employees, Todd liked to get an early start to his day. So when the plane struck at 8:46 a.m., Todd was trapped in the floors above the plane with no route to escape.

Todd's father worked in the same building on the 77th floor as an executive vice president of the World Trade Centers Association. He managed to make it out alive and survived the attacks. After suffering such a tremendous loss, Todd's parents sought a way to honor their only son's legacy. They created the Todd Ouida Children's Foundation (mybuddytodd.org), a living memorial to their late son.

For all his charm and outgoing nature, you'd never know that Todd had suffered from crippling childhood anxiety. The panic attacks were so debilitating that Todd could not attend a traditional school environment and had to be homeschooled for three-years. After years of research and effort, his family finally found a child psychologist who was able to help, but not before they became deeply troubled by the state of mental healthcare for children.

Now the foundation aims to help with research, treatment, and education of childhood anxiety disorders, having provided seven-figures in assistance to children and families to receive quality care.

Honoring Todd's commitment to the University of Michigan, his parents also created the Todd Ouida Clinical Scholars Award and Annual Lecture endowment. The Scholars Award annually funds young clinical psychology researchers who need access to private funding in order to conduct research and jumpstart their careers. The Annual Lecture brings prominent clinical psychology scholars from around the country to the University of Michigan's Depression Center every year to deliver educational talks on new research, ideas, and insights into the field of childhood psychology.

This living legacy throws its largest annual fundraiser every May in honor of Todd's birthday, always raising significant funds to help the cause. This birthday party celebrating a life cut short has received support from numerous corporate donors. Even Todd's favorite team, the New York Yankees, has been involved.

While Todd's parents tried to cope and make the best of the tragedy, I found myself reflecting on life's priorities. Todd was making a huge impact posthumously; I craved an outlet to make a difference now and have a greater impact on people's lives. Working in consulting was helping businesses become more efficient and profitable, but I wanted to do something bigger and more meaningful.

Todd was leaving a legacy to help others, and my father had left a legacy for his two sons (even if much of that financial legacy was ultimately unrealized). Helping people work with money, I thought, would have a positive effect and would help others avoid what happened to me. It took me a while to get all the finance industry licenses, but by the beginning of 2002, I'd made the move. I was going to help others create their own legacies.

I started out in the financial services industry working for a large national insurance company. I didn't know exactly what I was getting myself into, but I should've had an inkling—just before I started working there, the head of that office committed suicide so his family could collect his life insurance money. Talk about a huge red flag. That wasn't the kind of legacy I was interested in helping people achieve, and I left that firm within a few months.

After earning the professional licenses to offer both insurance and investments, I moved from the insurance firm to Citigroup, the largest investment company in the U.S., and the sixth largest corporation overall in the U.S. at the time. I dove deep into the new job, which really held my feet to the fire.

One of my first assignments was working with doctors and nurses at Detroit Medical Center (DMC), a large hospital in downtown Detroit with a network of facilities throughout the suburbs. I was seeing as many as fourteen people in a single day. I really liked helping people plan for retirement. I did very well there, often the first one to arrive and the last one to leave. I was passionate and driven. Despite being one of the youngest advisors, I became the top retirement plan counselor in the country for Citigroup's healthcare division. The company even sent me to a fancy conference in Bermuda to accept my award in front of all the big wigs. But by the time I went on stage to accept that award, I already knew I'd be leaving the big firm to make a major change.

Just before that conference, I was brought into a conference room in my Detroit-based office. Three superiors in fancy suits sat at the table. "We believe you would make a great fit in executive leadership here." I was flattered and proud that my hard work was being acknowledged, especially so early in my career. But following an executive trajectory meant that I would be mentoring other advisors, not interacting directly with clients. I wasn't so sure about that.

I asked about the key responsibilities. That's when I learned that my role would primarily be pushing specific investments on my advisors. I asked why those specific investments. They told me, "Because those are the best ones, of course."

Being curious by nature, I was not satisfied with that response. My superiors seemed to genuinely believe that we were recommending the best investments available, but they could not give any sound reasoning behind their selection process. They simply accepted the information that their superiors provided them. I was cut from a different cloth.

I told them I needed to think about their proposal. I immediately began investigating how my firm determined which investments were "the best." I expected to come across lengthy analytics, or reports highlighting key performance metrics, or some sort of client-focused numerical selection criteria. Instead, I discovered that our firm was choosing their preferred funds not for their quality, not for the best interests of the client, but for what made the highest profits for the firm. I learned the specifics of kickback arrangements and profit sharing, where funds literally pay the firm money to sell their investment offerings over those of their competitors. This meant bigger bonuses and commissions. It was a giant propaganda scheme from the top-down, designed to trick all the advisors into believing that we were designing the industry's best portfolios so the clients would buy into that same belief system.

I had an epiphany. All this time at the big firm, I genuinely believed that I was helping people build excellent retirement plans. Turns out I was actually the company's pawn, a voice-box to inflate the firm's pockets. I never questioned the company's leadership when they said that we should be recommending mutual fund ABC and variable annuity XYZ to our clients.

I was sick to my stomach and wanted out. There had to be a better way to be a financial advisor without compromising my morals.

Even though I was helping people build their financial plans, I was working as a registered representative—not a fiduciary. That meant that I simply needed to confirm that investments were *suitable* for their situation. In other words, if the investment was not *unsuitable*, then it was fine to recommend. This meant I could steer clients toward "approved funds," where my company would receive a bonus, kickbacks, or other incentives from the mutual fund company. Over time, I found that many financial professionals work purely on commission and are always stressed about where their next paycheck is coming from. Making that next sale is the difference between taking that family vacation or staying home.

Even though I was doing very well financially, I began to realize that the big financial services companies don't care about their clients or even their advisors—as long as the money keeps rolling in and profits are maximized, they are content. In the end, I realized that my clients weren't being treated as individuals with their own aspirations and goals, but were being treated like a number. All the company cared about was whether I made my sales quota of whatever funds they were pushing at the time.

I always tried to do the right thing by my clients. I never wanted to pull the kinds of shady tricks that had drained my inheritance from my father. So I put in my notice at Citigroup and decided to charter a new path. My boss asked, "Are you sure? You have a career laid out for you here." I assured her my mind was made up. One last plea: "You're really going to leave your stock options behind?!" I said yes, I was.

I shared the news with my mom, a retired school teacher and librarian with a comfortable pension. She gasped, "You're going to leave the stability of your job with a pension?!" I said yes, I was.

Two-weeks later, I was unemployed but I was armed with time. I was armed with the ability to be patient. My prudent savings granted me the gift of carving my next career path strategically and with purpose.

When I left Citigroup, stock options were valued at $500 per share. After the stock market crashed in 2008, those stock options were valued at a mere $25 per share. Citi employees who were relying on those stock options watched their portfolio drop by 95% in just a few years' time.

My potential future pension that my mom so coveted was frozen on January 1, 2008 – a fortuitous sign of the times considering this was nine-months prior to the 2008 market crash. The days of retirement stability provided by employers were over.

As I pondered strategically over striking out on my own, I realized that I needed to reeducate myself to best serve my future clients. I learned that both clients and advisors are sold a lot of bad advice when it comes to retirement planning. But I've also learned that there is a better way to do retirement planning, and it starts by unlearning a lot of what the big financial services firms have told us and sold us over the years.

CHAPTER 2

Choosing a Financial Advisor

Most people never learn about investing, saving, or managing money in school, and some people never learn about it at all. If they do learn anything, it is often the bare minimum. There are always more pressing things to deal with than the myriad of questions surrounding investing and retirement planning.

So why do most people fail at reaching their retirement goals? It comes down to one word: *procrastination*. Planning for the future never has the same urgency as all the other more pressing things happening in our lives, whether it's defrosting the freezer, picking up the dry cleaning, or tending to bigger things like a career, kids, or caring for an elderly parent.

Why Wait?

On average, most people put more time into planning their next vacation than planning their retirement years. And the most common reasons I find are they don't know how, and they don't know where to start.

It doesn't help that long-range retirement planning can be boring. Most people don't enjoy going through a bunch of numbers, and there's the difficulty of doing it all yourself. It's a lot like trying to do your own taxes, except that with taxes, you're only looking at one year of your financial life—and you have a hard and fast deadline. Now imagine that the whole process is more complicated, covers thirty years of your life, and there's no deadline. People tell themselves, "It'll be OK in the future," or "It will work itself out," or

"I'll figure it out when the time comes." No wonder people tend to procrastinate!

The reality is that a lot of people never take the time to do any retirement planning. They reach a certain point and say, "I need money so I'll start collecting Social Security now." That's literally their entire retirement plan—whatever they can get from Social Security. And if they're fortunate and smart enough to have saved well over the years, they simply hope and pray those retirement savings will last.

What's interesting is that this endless procrastination is usually not about fear. Many people are not concerned about having enough money to retire, or that they won't be able to retire, or even that they're afraid of making a mistake with their financial plan. It's simply not knowing where to start, and then getting frustrated and bored and feeling it's not helping them or it's too overwhelming.

Most people start retirement planning by trying to figure it out on their own. They don't understand what financial planners and retirement planners do and how that is different than a do-it-yourself approach. It's actually relatively easy for retirement planners to take your information and immediately understand financial details and options that you never would have discovered on your own, because this is the information they have seen and examined every day for years. And these insights can mean huge financial advantages to you.

There's also an intimidation factor that comes from the big financial services firms, which makes retirement planning sound like some gigantic technical mystery. You know the firms I'm talking about; they all operate essentially the same. These firms make retirement planning seem so complicated that you wouldn't possibly understand, so just give them all your money, trust them to look after your interests, and you'll find out whether or not they did a good job some number of years from now. That works to the advantage of the big-name planning firms. They can flex their big names and marketing budgets. People have heard of them and they seem familiar, and that's about as much research as some people do to find a planner. They have no clue whether those firms are actually doing a good job.

Some of my favorite clients to help are the ones who say, "I don't know what I don't know." These folks are usually pretty savvy when it comes to finance and investing. They feel like they've done a good job over the years of researching which mutual funds to select in their

401(k) or picking out stocks in a brokerage account. But when they realize the expertise of a true professional, the bulb lights up and they understand there is much more nuance to the puzzle than they originally thought. What they need is more guidance: guidance to identify and create solutions for the investment aspects they didn't even know existed. This is when I can best help, because I can provide a much more comprehensive plan and portfolio, which ultimately means increasing the likelihood of a successful retirement, whatever those individual goals may be.

One thing that should motivate people to start thinking about retirement investing sooner rather than later, is that they could be missing out on free money. Literally, *free money*.

When I worked with hospital employees at DMC, I held weekly meetings for newly-hired employees to explain their 403(b)/401(k) plans. I told them, "Make sure you're getting your free money!" While it may not sound like much, the hospital provided a 100-percent match on the first two-percent of contributions. This is an immediate 100-percent gain right off the bat! The next two-percent in contributions received a 50-percent match, an immediate 50-percent gain. So on the first four-percent of retirement plan contributions, employees would get an immediate 3-percent match. All they had to do was get started.

While this may surprise some people, the reality is that most employees across America are not maxing out their matching money in their 401(k)s. If you're thinking this is akin to throwing away money, you're right!

My clients often ask me what advice I would give to their young professional children just starting to save. My reply always starts the same: Make sure they are maxing out the match on their 401(k) plan! That matching money compounded with time makes an incredible difference in terms of how much of a nest egg they can create before they retire.

This is a major difference with my work now: We work with people on a much more personal level. I get to know the families beyond the names on the accounts. I can help my clients' children and other loved ones set themselves up for successful futures. When I was working at Citigroup, it was very transactional. *How much do you want to save per pay period? When would you like to retire so we know which of five pre-determined portfolios to stick your money into? Who are your beneficiaries and how do you want to split your money between them?* We didn't get to know the people and their circumstances. When I left that job, I was then able to concentrate on spending more time truly getting to know people on a personal level. This allowed me to understand how a family's financials need to be the vehicle by which they can realize their goals and dreams. Money for the sake of money is corporate; money for the sake of life fulfillment and enjoyment is the key to success.

I want to know what makes people happy. If you'd like to spend time with your grandkids in California, we want to make sure we're budgeting that in as part of your lifestyle. Do you want to take the extended family on a trip to Disney World? Great, let's make sure that's in the plan. Maybe you want a trip to Europe every summer or a winter home on the water in Florida? Perfect, we will structure a plan to realize those goals.

While some clients have no problem spending their hard-earned money and I need to reel in their spending, I find it's often quite the opposite. Some families actually need encouraging that it's okay to spend their money. For those who have spent their entire working lives saving for retirement, it can be challenging to suddenly feel like it's okay to spend from that same nest egg. But when people can see their overall financial plan and how that spending fits within it, that's when the true rewards of a lifetime of responsible saving can be enjoyed.

In the end, I do my job better – and it's more satisfying – when I get personally involved in understanding the lives of my clients. And that's led to us helping out our clients' parents, children, and other loved ones. Often times, people ask us, "I know my kids don't have a lot of money, but would you be willing to help them?"

I say, "Of course, we're happy to help and be of any assistance that we can." So, it's a much deeper connection on a more emotional level. We have a personal relationship together, and even though we're doing very advanced and sophisticated planning, I think that the emotional connection is really the biggest differentiator and what our clients appreciate most.

Differentiating Between Advisors

The financial world has done a really bad job of differentiating between the various types of financial professionals, and I strongly believe that's intentional. The big Wall Street firms would rather have their financial professionals do whatever their bosses want them to do, or whatever their shareholders want them to do, rather than have more stringent requirements, such as a fiduciary rule. The big firms make it very difficult for investors to know the difference between say, a Certified Life Underwriter and a Chartered Financial Analyst, and whether it even matters for their situation.

If an advisor is truly acting as a fiduciary, it means that person has a legal and ethical responsibility to act in the client's best interests, putting the client's interests first and foremost in every decision that advisor makes. If a fiduciary advisor is choosing an investment for your money, he or she cannot be swayed by the fact that one fund pays a higher commission than the other. Instead, he or she must choose the investment that's best for you. Again, this is an ethical and legal *obligation* with real consequences if not followed.

The vast majority of people don't even know what a fiduciary is. There needs to be more awareness about not only the definition of *fiduciary*, but how to find one and how to distinguish the real thing from the impersonators. The bottom line is this: having a fiduciary reduces conflicts of interest that exist between what the advisor recommendations to you and how that advisor gets paid. Does it mean that all fiduciaries avoid conflicts of interest? Probably not. But if a fiduciary ever wrongs you, you have legal recourse at your disposal, unlike with other advisor types.

Often times, advisors garner a collection of acronyms to display after their name on a business card. This can involve little more than paying to join a certification group or paying to attend a training conference. Then suddenly, over the course of a weekend, they've amassed a bunch of letters following their name that may look impressive to an unaware eye. Many times, those letters are just a front.

Even something as seemingly respectable as the CFP® designation - CERTIFIED FINANCIAL PLANNER® - leaves a bad taste in my mouth. For years, the CFP Board created an impression through their marketing that CFP® professionals are fiduciaries, when in fact, this was not the case. After years of controversy, the CFP board finally established a requirement that CFP® professionals act as fiduciaries "at all times" beginning July 1, 2020. The fact that the CFP Board deliberately lobbied against the fiduciary standard for so many years, and frankly manipulated and deceived the public, made the designation forever unappealing to those of us "in the know." This is why I intentionally avoided obtaining the CFP® designation.

It's a fuzzy line that the CFP Board has created, because even though it's a much more demanding credential than a weekend course, it still doesn't tell people if you are actually a fiduciary. In fact, some states have considered legislation banning advisors from using the CFP® designation altogether. Back in 2018, the state of Missouri passed legislation banning just that, but CFP lobbyists appealed to Washington to make sure that never materialized.[1]

There are only two licenses for financial advisors—the Series 65 and Series 66 license—that require the advisor to work under the fiduciary standard. But it's still not as simple as that. The problem is that an advisor can have a Series 65 or 66 license and combine it with a non-fiduciary registered representative license like a Series 7. This is what most of the big firms have their advisors do. That way, the advisor can claim to be a fiduciary, but if you ever rightfully claim they were not acting in your best interests, they can say, "Oh, I was not acting as a fiduciary when I gave you that recommendation. I gave you that recommendation in my capacity as a registered representative." Basically, it creates a big loophole where an advisor can claim to be a fiduciary, but they don't actually have to follow any fiduciary rules. It is a huge conflict of interest.

Personally, I gave up all of my registered representative licenses when I went off on my own. I wanted to be a true fiduciary so I dropped the licenses the big firms made me get, and I got a Series 65 as my only investment license. Now when I make a recommendation to a client, I am acting in a fiduciary capacity only. What it really comes down to, is that even if an advisor has one of those fiduciary licenses, you still have to find somebody you can trust and who offers a reasonable investment strategy. And if that advisor has a fiduciary

---

[1] Ann Marsh. Financial Planning. August 16, 2018. "CFP Board, FPA get busy after Missouri bans CFP designation." https://www.financial-planning.com/news/cfp-board-fpa-join-pcc-to-halt-states-from-harming-cfps

license (Series 65 or 66) and additional licenses, you have to be willing to accept the risks that the advisor may not be acting as a fiduciary at all times, and that if that advisor wrongs you, there may be no legal recourse.

The industry has been blurring the lines for years, making it difficult for people to understand the difference between which advisors are fiduciaries and which ones aren't. You can go to BrokerCheck.com, the website run by the private Financial Industry Regulatory Authority (FINRA), where consumers can check on advisors and brokers. But even there, it's not entirely clear whether an advisor is exclusively a fiduciary or not. In order to tell, enter an advisor's name in the search bar. When their result comes up, it will show whether they are an Investment Advisor Representative (aka Fiduciary), a Registered Representative (aka a Broker), or if they hold both licenses. If an advisor is exclusively a fiduciary, BrokerCheck will redirect you to the Securities and Exchange Commission (SEC) website, which is the governing body that oversees fiduciary advisors. But how many people would know to do this? How would they know that Investment Advisor Representative is an official term for fiduciary, and that the word Broker is synonymous with Registered Representative (i.e., non-fiduciary)? Most people would never know the difference.

Check the Advisor's Disclosures & Experience

In my opinion, the biggest factor in selecting an advisor is finding a true fiduciary, but another important consideration is checking the advisor's disclosures, which is a listing of client complaints against the advisor.

I'll often mention to people that looking up an advisor on BrokerCheck.com is an important thing to do. I have had people report back to me how shocked they were by the disclosures listed on BrokerCheck against their current advisor. One woman came back to me who was working with an advisor at Chase Bank who had nine disclosures against her while being licensed for under ten years. That is nearly one every year! How is that even possible? I've worked in the finance industry since 2002—and I have zero. It would be hard to pick up nine.

Another disclosure to watch out for is bankruptcy. Now, bankruptcy can happen to anyone who's come upon hard times. But in general, you probably want a financial advisor who's fairly financially savvy in their own life, to give you money management advice.

Disclosures also report any legal and criminal history for the advisor. I have seen advisors have disclosures showing history of domestic violence, drug possession, and DUIs. While this may not be directly related to managing investments, I believe it is an indication of character. It is information you can take and decide how much weight it carries when selecting an advisor to manage your life savings.

I've had people report to me and tell me that they looked me up on BrokerCheck.com. I've been told that my profile "is pretty boring." I like to keep my profile boring and consider that a compliment! I think most people would agree that you probably don't want to have a lot of drama with the person who is handling your money.

Another thing to consider when choosing an advisor is their level of experience and how established their business is. I'll be frank: Financial advising can be a very well-paying profession, but that is only true of the top-tier of professionals. To make a good living, advisors need to have an established client base. When advisors are starting out and building their practice, their next paycheck is directly tied to whether you become a client. The risk of conflicts of interest is huge.

I remember starting out and the frustration of not having a decent payday in months. Thankfully, I was in a position where I had comfortable savings under my belt. I could sustain myself financially while I built my business. This is the exception, not the norm. I have heard advisors admit in professional circles that they recommended investment products to their clients solely based on highest commission, because they didn't know when their next paycheck would come along.

In general, you want an advisor with a number of years of experience under his or her belt. The experienced advisor with a strong client base should no longer feel the financial desperation that a less established advisor feels.

Another hidden danger is that almost all of the big advisory firms enforce strict quotas on their advisors. Even though an advisor at a big firm may no longer face the pressure of earning an income, they do face the continual pressure of losing their job if their quotas are not met. In contrast, independent advisors and management groups don't have to keep anyone happy but their clients.

Sometimes I hear things like, "How do I know you're not Bernie Madoff? How do I know you won't take my money for yourself?" This is a really easy trap to avoid, as long as you understand what to look for. A huge red flag is being told to write a check directly to your advisor, their company, or a company you've never heard of and cannot find enough verifying information about them (i.e., a fictitious company your advisor created to appear like a legitimate investment company). In a properly managed firm, your money goes to a third-party custodian, who is responsible for holding the client's money. The custodian provides a platform for the advisor to buy and sell investments without having access to the money. For example, my clients don't write a check to me or Wealth Trac, but to TD Ameritrade, Schwab, or Fidelity, all large, well-known institutions. I employ these custodians to provide an additional level of security and oversight. Bernie Madoff did not use a third-party custodian.

What to Look for in an Advisor

I'd say the top four things to look for in an advisor are:

1. They work under the fiduciary standard where they're required to put your best interests first, which means they most likely stay away from the big investment companies because of all the incompatible incentives and conflicts of interest.

2. The advisor has a clean record with no disclosures or minimal disclosures and no lawsuits. If there are disclosures, they are minor and hopefully from many years ago, and the advisor disclosed them to you from the start.

3. They use a custodian so you're not investing directly with the advisor or their firm. This protects your money.

4. A final consideration is whether any potential advisor fully answers all your questions. You want to work with someone who does not talk over your head. Somebody speaking in technical jargon might be hiding things by glossing over a full explanation, because they think you won't understand what they're talking about. This can be a form of intimidation. I almost never need to use financial jargon with a client. It's important that an advisor keeps things simple enough for the average person to understand. The better you understand your investments, the better decisions you will make, and the more comfortable and confident you will feel with your financial situation.

Fee Models

There are several types of fee models offered by financial advisors these days. They can be tricky to distinguish from one another. And even trickier is figuring out which fee model is best for each type of investor. You also need to be aware of the services that are being provided for the fee, and the inherent conflicts of interest with how that advisor is getting paid. Paying for a financial advisor is very much a case of "You get what you pay for."

The most common way of paying an advisor is fee-based. This is when an advisor is paid a fixed percentage of your invested assets, typically in the one-percent to two-percent range. The advisor's fee is automatically paid from the accounts on either a monthly or quarterly basis. This fee model keeps the advisor's interests in line with your interests. As your portfolio increases, so does the advisor's paycheck. If your portfolio decreases, the advisor's paycheck goes down. In this model, the advisor has every incentive to make sure your portfolio is optimized and performing as it should. You and the advisor are in a partnership where you both want the portfolio to grow and be protected.

As a fiduciary, I believe this model is the most logical and sound approach. This model has other benefits, such as providing access to investments that are not readily available to the general public, such as separately managed accounts, which are like creating your own personalized funds.

However, there are caveats with fee-based arrangements, as well. Consider the big firms using cookie-cutter portfolios that are not personalized to your situation whatsoever. You answer some questions about your anticipated retirement date and your risk tolerance. Then you get put into one of four or five portfolios that company offers. Yet you're still paying a percentage of your portfolio to the advisor month after month, year after year. This is a case of not getting value out of the fee you're paying.

This can even be true of large independent advisory firms. Some big-name advisors have a stream of media commitments: a syndicated radio show, a series of published books, an active YouTube or other social media channel, and a team of advisors and sub-advisors reporting to them. Advisors in firms like these may not be their own thinkers. In order to serve the vast number of clients they serve, they may operate just like the big firms by offering just a handful of model portfolios. Then they simply plug clients into the one they see fit.

Whether big or small, these types of cookie-cutter firms rarely deviate from those pre-packaged portfolios. Due to the volume of clients they serve, they must have a consistent investment philosophy across the company, regardless of the individual advisor or client. That means you're not getting individual advice. You're essentially working with a salesperson, a representative who can sell you a model portfolio, then the portfolio goes on autopilot once you sign on the dotted line.

Keep in mind, my strong belief is that a fee-based model is the best way to protect client interests. But it's the client's responsibility to understand the value they're getting from their fee. One advisor could offer fully customized portfolios, whereas another advisor is sticking you in a one-sized-fits-all portfolio. You're paying the same model for both levels of service, so make sure you understand what you're paying for and how to get the best value for your fee.

Another fee model that has become more prevalent in recent years is the fee-only model. While it sounds similar to fee-based, it is very different.

Fee-only advisors charge an hourly fee for their services, usually in the $150 to $500 per hour range, plus a start-up cost in the $1,500 to $5,000 range. With fee-only advisors, clients may pay more or less than fee-based advisors. It depends how much time the advisor dedicates to your portfolio. If the advisor spends too much time, you may be overcharged. If the advisor spends too little time, you save money but may lack attention and quality advice. The greatest incentive a fee-based advisor has is the amount of time they can bill.

The relationship with a fee-only advisor can be very transactional. They make a recommendation for your portfolio, but you might be responsible for implementing it. That means the fee-only advisor generally recommends common investments that are readily available to the general public.

There is a lot of misinformation out there about whether fee-based or fee-only is better. Frankly, I have found even reputable websites get the terms confused and spread misinformation as a result. For example, a reputable website I will leave unnamed, stated that fee-only advisors are fiduciaries and fee-based advisors are not. In fact, fiduciaries and non-fiduciaries can utilize either fee-structure. There is no direct relationship between billing structure and being a fiduciary. And if it were related, I would argue that it is more appropriate for a fiduciary to utilize a fee-based model where the incentive is how well your portfolio does, as opposed to a fee-only model where the incentive is connected to how much time they can bill.

In my experience, clients wanting comprehensive financial planning are better served with a fee-based advisor. Clients wanting occasional advice they can implement themselves may be better served with a fee-only advisor.

In recent years, the robo-advisor concept has gained momentum, as well. This is investing in a portfolio managed by a computer algorithm. Returns tend to match typical market returns. Robo-advisors cannot create comprehensive financial plans. They are cost-effective, but again, you get what you pay for. This can be a decent option for young, busy professionals looking to get into investing.

When looking for a financial professional, you should meet with them for a general interview about their approach to investing, their experience working with clients in similar circumstances to you, and an overall idea of how they would handle your assets and investment goals. This should help you understand whether they are hands-on or hands-off, and whether you'd be getting what you want out of the relationship.

While you may be considering this an opportunity to interview your potential future advisor, the advisor should also be interviewing you, their potential future client. Any established, responsible advisor should not take on every person who walks through the door. Just as you weigh the decision to take on an advisor, that advisor should also determine whether your situation and goals align well with their investment philosophy and whether it's a good personality fit.

During this initial meeting, you should not be asked to pay anything, but you also shouldn't expect any specific recommendations at this point, either. And, of course, you should consider how completely a potential advisor answers your questions.

Communications with an Advisor

In terms of communicating with an advisor, we usually meet face-to-face with our clients annually, and we're in regular contact over phone, email, and through our client newsletters and updates. Some clients like to schedule a yearly meeting and stick to that same schedule for years, like an annual physical at the doctor's office. Others don't want to meet unless it is urgent. The reality is that many people don't like dealing with their finances, which is sometimes why they hired us in the first place. In some cases, our clients have relocated far away from our office. (Of course, virtual meetings have made long-distance communication much easier.)

Over time, I've found that almost all clients are content coming to our group market update presentations and receiving monthly statements, progress reports, and newsletters from my firm. It's rare, but I've had some clients who haven't met with us one-on-one in years, call me up and say, "I'm retiring in a year, so let's get together to talk now." The fact that we haven't met personally in a while frankly doesn't matter because we've been communicating through other forms, and we're always monitoring our clients' portfolios. The point is that communication can be customized to whatever best fits with that client's preferences.

Even if we're on an annual face-to-face schedule with a client, our firm is always available. If something comes up and we need to schedule a visit or a phone call, we accommodate that without hesitation.

The point of a yearly visit is to check in personally, make sure the financial plan is still optimized, and to see if any life situations have come up that require us to tweak or reconsider the plan.

I know of some advisory firms that require advisors to meet with the same client four times per year. There is no particular reason for those meetings other than solidifying the relationship. These advisors say it's a struggle to come up with content to discuss, and the clients come to resent the frequent meetings because there is little accomplished during that time. Meeting for the sake of meeting is not productive for anyone.

Once you've found an advisor you trust to work with, and you've agreed on a strategy and investment approach, your portfolio may be thought of as more "set it and forget it" since the management of the accounts is being handled without your constant involvement. Unless you have some kind of significant life change, like getting married, having children, or getting ready to retire, a good investment plan can allow you to ignore your accounts. This means you can spend your time doing things you enjoy rather than worrying about your money. In most cases, our clients feel free to ignore the ups and downs of the stock market or the world economic scene because they know that we are watching their investments and managing their accounts. When the market goes down, we don't get bombarded with calls and emails from concerned clients. That's because we have a plan for our clients and they know it. Our investment plans offer lower volatility than other advisors' plans, and our clients understand the individual strategy we've created for them. If you understand the plan and the plan is in place, then you will feel comfortable.

One of the most important times I sit down with my clients is in connection with significant life events. Typically, the most significant event people want to plan for is their retirement. They want to develop a plan to retire so they feel confident and comfortable with that decision. Most people are shooting from the hip when they think they can retire—they're just guessing. Many of the people I meet are actually in a better situation than they thought. When we put together a plan, we can show them how long their money will last. Many times, people's reaction is, "Wow! We didn't know we had that much stability."

Feeling Comfortable and Confident About Retirement

Arming people with financial knowledge is such an important and fulfilling purpose for me. We often see people around the age of sixty who tell us their goal is to retire at sixty-five. When we provide them knowledge about finances and explain where they stand, we're sometimes able to tell them they can retire earlier than expected. That's a great feeling. When people move up their retirement date based solely on the knowledge and the information we've given them, I really take pride in our ability to help.

Many people think worst-case scenario when it comes to expectations about when they can stop working. Some worry about outliving their money. The reality is that retirees spend money in waves. In my opinion, retirees should make sure to enjoy some of their money early in retirement. That's when people feel the most active and healthy compared to later in retirement. Go ahead and travel, take up hobbies, do the things that you may not be able to do later on.

Inflation will have an impact on spending amounts throughout retirement, but this is another area where people sometimes assume the worst. You may find an inflation or retirement calculator that shows if you're spending $6,000 a month when you're sixty-five, you should expect to spend $12,000 a month when you're ninety. But that's rarely the case. Unless you need constant care, my experience supports that you'll spend much less at age ninety compared to now. Nevertheless, we always factor various rates of inflation into our analyses and retirement plans so we are prepared for the worst.

With a proper financial strategy in place, we can show people exactly how much they can expect to spend in retirement without carrying around the concern that their money may run out.

In that regard, I love to see people spend their money and enjoy the rewards of a lifetime of hard work and responsible saving. Being able to give people more confidence that they're going to be okay in retirement, allows them to feel safe spending a bit more freely. Financial freedom in retirement is what everybody wants.

David Bach, author of *The Automatic Millionaire* and eight other New York Times Best Sellers, noticed some big investment companies talk only about ROI—return on investment. "What is the ROI on your investments?" But Bach talks about ROR, which is "return on retirement." He emphasizes having a happy retirement, not just focusing on investment returns.

People don't have to worry about outperforming the market or the ROI of their investments if they have a strategy that works for them.

Tax Planning for Retirement

One important consideration that a good advisor considers—but most clients never think about—is tax planning. While you're still working and in the accumulation phase of investing, you were focused on putting money away in your 401(k). You probably were not thinking about how that disciplined approach to saving would impact your tax situation in the future.

Taking money out of retirement accounts when you retire is a huge part of your return on retirement. This is another area where it's not just about ROI. How much are you actually getting for retirement after the government gets its cut? The way you take distributions, how you take required withdrawals, paying attention to staying within your tax bracket, all of these things are very important.

That's why in retirement, there should be a portfolio shift toward consistently generating income. That means having more dividend-paying investments, lowering the volatility of your portfolio, and being able to take money from different tax buckets if the market goes down. The pre-retirement accumulation phase can be pretty easy—you just ride the wave, automatically contributing and investing. You can't do that once you're retired. Every year is important. You need to go from looking at things with a time horizon of decades to structuring it on more of a year-by-year approach in retirement.

In the accumulation phase, you have more time to bounce back from a mistake. When you're working, you will still be okay financially during a volatile down market period because you're still generating a consistent income, and you have time on your side. But if you make that mistake after you stop working, things suddenly become very different. You get one shot at retirement. One mistake can mean huge losses, which can range in consequences from leaving less behind to your heirs or charities, to losing your financial freedom.

Red Flags to Look Out For

Offices like mine can provide a full range of financial options, but that's not the case with all financial professionals. Certain designations allow people to provide specific product offerings. Many who call themselves "financial advisors" are only permitted to sell insurance. The term *financial advisor* is not specific to any training, degree, or designation; it is a phrase that literally anyone can slap on a business card and use.

Take my company, for instance. We have all the licenses that enable us to recommend virtually the entire universe of financial offerings, which we pick and choose between to customize plans for individuals and families. We do tax planning, healthcare planning, income planning, and estate planning, in addition to the obvious investment planning. There are many titles that could be used to describe our advisors, and *financial advisor* is certainly one of them.

Now take an insurance agent. Once you reach a certain age, you will notice that you begin receiving lots of invitations to attend free dinner seminars. You agree to listen to a financial presentation, and you get a free meal at a nice restaurant in exchange. These seminars are often led by insurance agents with no additional licenses. This means they can only offer insurance products, not securities investments. They cannot manage a portfolio, for example. Now, these presenters are fully able to call themselves financial advisors, just as I can call myself a financial advisor. But there is a world of difference between the two types of advisors, but most people are unaware. After all, it is the same title.

Let's say that you agree to meet with that financial advisor from the dinner seminar. I am willing to bet that advisor is going to offer you an annuity and nothing else. They are generally a one-trick pony. Would you trust your life savings with someone who can only offer one piece of the puzzle? If someone is offering you an annuity on its own without additional investment recommendations, this is a red flag.

At a very basic level, before you even get into the fiduciary stuff, insurance-only advisors are out there to sell you insurance. Now, insurance is very complicated if you get into using life insurance appropriately for estate planning reasons and tax-free income. But these more complex strategies are almost always paired with other strategies utilizing securities as part of a comprehensive financial plan. Someone who is only able to recommend insurance ends up recommending only the most basic of insurance strategies. In my mind, insurance-only advice is working with half a deck, and insurance-only advisors who call themselves financial advisors are not really financial advisors.

Another red flag is a financial professional who possesses an investment license, but does not utilize it. If a fully licensed advisor is only recommending an annuity, for example, that professional is not using their investment licenses in any capacity. Sometimes a financial professional will take their investment exams simply to give the appearance of being a comprehensive advisor, or to be able to call themselves a fiduciary. But if that advisor is only offering you an annuity or a life insurance policy, for example, this could be a clue that the advisor is not interested in utilizing their fiduciary license or offering comprehensive financial planning.

Another red flag is meeting with two different advisors at the same firm, who present two different investment offerings. Perhaps you're sitting in a room with two advisors, or you meet with one and then with another advisor at a different time. One may be a fully licensed fiduciary, while the other is an insurance specialist or a broker (non-fiduciary). You may see the advisors switch between who's talking or who is giving what recommendation, based on whether or not they want to give you advice that adheres to the fiduciary standard. This is a red flag.

Another thing I regularly see is cookie-cutter portfolios, especially from the big-name investment management companies. I understand how this happens. With tons of accounts to manage, the big firms have to maximize efficiency. Therefore, people end up in one of several pre-determined portfolios. You answer a risk questionnaire, it spits out your number, and then you're put into

Portfolio X. While this may benefit the company by maximizing efficiency, it does not necessarily benefit the client.

This cookie-cutter approach ignores any tax strategy, which is critically important, especially in retirement. If all your assets have the same risk tolerance, then it's probably not a complex enough strategy.

What I mean by that is, we invest money differently between taxable accounts, Individual Retirement Accounts, and Roth IRA accounts. Those investments are in three different tax categories. Besides being in different tax buckets, those investments also are in different time-horizon buckets. You cannot take a one-size-fits-all approach to using those accounts.

With a Roth IRA, for example, we invest more aggressively because we're using that as a longer-term asset. You don't necessarily want to take that same approach when you use a taxable investment account.

Not only should the risk levels be different across your various accounts, you also need to take into account the frequency of trades within the taxable account. Every time a trade is made within a taxable account, it creates a taxable event. The same is not true with a Roth IRA.

To summarize, here is some info to expand on how to determine if there is something "wrong" with your relationship with your advisor. The main red flags that come to mind are:

1. **Too much trading.** Trading can happen, but it shouldn't be too frequent. On tax-qualified accounts, trading can be more frequent because there are no tax consequences with trading. I will use more "tactical" strategies in qualified accounts, and more passive strategies in non-qualified accounts.

2. **Fees you can't understand, and that the advisor won't explain to you.** I actually had a client say that their advisor said, "Don't worry about the fees. They are low." If you're not willing to explain it, I don't really believe it.

3. **If you ask them if they are a fiduciary, they give a long, drawn-out answer that basically walks around the whole topic.** If that's the case, the answer likely is NO, they are not a fiduciary or are not exclusively a fiduciary.

4. **They don't follow through.** You wouldn't believe the number of times that I hear from a client that their advisor told them they would do an income analysis for them, then they never hear back. If you ask this of me, I will schedule a time right then and there to review this analysis with you. If my team has a week, we can get it done.

5. **The advisor tells you there are certain investments that you are not "allowed" to buy or hold.** There are firms out there that say you aren't allowed to buy some very commonly traded ETF investments. I had a client who owned a certain cybersecurity ETF. They told him he had to sell it. He asked why? They told him it was too risky. That was clearly not the case for this individual. The real explanation was that the advisory firm wasn't getting kickbacks on it anymore, so they said it was too risky.

Choosing your financial advisor is a crucially important step in retirement readiness, so don't make that choice lightly. Even if a friend or relative has a great experience with an advisor, don't assume that advisor will be the right person for you.

I know people hate thinking about the nuts and bolts of retirement because it means they're aging, but the fact is: you can either age with your finances a mess, or you can age with your money well-managed so that your retirement is a comfortable one.

Until you get ready to retire, investing can be relatively simple—you invest money regularly, you let time work on your side, and, if something bad happens, you still have time to recover and rebuild your finances. Once you stop getting a regular income and start depending on your retirement savings, things get much more complicated—and carry much higher stakes because you only get one chance to get your retirement right.

That's why you should talk to an advisor, ask lots of questions, and use the information in this chapter to help you choose an advisor who can help provide the retirement you deserve.

CHAPTER 3

It's Not What You Make, It's What You Keep

Making a lot of money doesn't guarantee that you're going to be able to build a comfortable retirement nest egg or achieve any of your other financial goals if you're regularly spending too much money. In fact, people with modest incomes can be very successful financially, while those with big incomes who act like big spenders can come up short.

Many of us can take lessons from our grandparents who lived during the Depression. I remember that even though my grandmother lived in a very nice house outside of Washington, D.C., she'd save her napkin from one meal to the next—a habit she developed during the 1920s and 1930s when even one extra nickel could make a difference in the household.

Money Mindfulness

Being wasteful never makes financial sense. Finding ways to free up cash in your budget not only allows you to invest and save more, but also gives you protection from financial shocks or economic downturns. Having more cash to invest also allows you to take less risk while staying on track to meet your financial goals. That's why bestselling author David Bach coined the term "latte factor"—a seemingly harmless indulgence like spending $4 on fancy coffee. If too many little luxuries turn into frequent habits, several lattés a day adds up to thousands of dollars in a year and much, much more when compounded over two or three decades.

One of the best money habits you can develop is mindfulness—the awareness of our thoughts and reactions in the moment–which isn't only a healthy mental habit but a financially rewarding one, too. Rather than budgeting and tracking every dime your family spends, being money-mindful means being aware of where your money goes while recognizing your realities and establishing your own individual financial priorities.

At a basic level, that's just part of learning to live within your means. But in a larger sense, it's also about the role you choose for money in your life. More financial experts are emphasizing the value of life experiences over material possessions. Your money can bring you a collection of bright shiny stuff, or it can give you the time and freedom to make your own decisions, whether it's leaving an unfulfilling job or contributing to your favorite charity.

A big priority in my own life is traveling. One of the most memorable experiences was visiting the nation of Laos, where the average income for a villager is as little as $1 a day. I found people were extremely happy, even if they didn't have the latest gadget. In fact, we traveled to a remote village with no electricity. Visiting this village required an eight-hour boat ride down the Mekong River. Needless to say, that village rarely gets visitors. When we pulled out a smartphone to snap a picture, the villagers gasped. They had literally never seen a smartphone in their lives. They were mesmerized and intrigued, but this fancy technology couldn't make them any happier than they already were with their simple lives.

This was an important reminder of how little we need in terms of material possessions to get along in life and be happy, and that even in today's modern world, there are people living vastly different lives than what we experience every day.

Experiences like these remind me that I would much rather spend money to create memories and life lessons with my family than to spend money on more frivolous things.

Some of the richest people in the nation end up miserable and in big trouble because they neglect the importance of paying attention to their money. Consider all the multi-millionaire athletes who went broke after becoming big spenders, or the actor Johnny Depp who blamed his financial advisors for his money problems, despite his own decision to buy and maintain fourteen luxury homes.[2] The lesson is that you need to pay attention to your money and live within your means, no matter how much money you make. Money only solves the most basic problems in life—the rest is up to you.

Evaluating Your Lifestyle

My clients are in the fortunate position where they don't need budgeting help, and they aren't living paycheck to paycheck. That's when it becomes easy to start thinking about elevating lifestyle. It's easy to start considering purchasing the newest, hottest item. But one thing I've noticed about really wealthy people: they usually are not eager to make flashy purchases for the latest, greatest thing.

You'd be surprised how many millionaires drive used cars. Sam Walton, founder of Walmart, bought a Ford F150 in 1979 that became his vehicle of choice. In his words, "I just don't believe a big showy lifestyle is appropriate. Why do I drive a pickup truck? What am I supposed to haul my dogs around in, a Rolls Royce?"[3]

From a financial standpoint, buying a two-year-old used car instead of the current model means you're not taking the huge hit in depreciation, which can be as much as one-third of the price. That value disappears the minute you drive that car off the lot, but you're still paying for it. Often times, a two- or three-year old used car looks exactly the same as the newest model. If you can find one that has been well looked after with low mileage, you can enjoy that car at a steep discount.

It's really about deciding what are the most important things to you in your life? What really brings you happiness? If your lifelong heart's desire is to drive a fancy convertible, and it's something that you will appreciate and value every time you turn that key in the ignition, then that's a justifiable purchase assuming that it is affordable for your specific situation.

---

[2] Mark Seal. Vanity Fair. July 5, 2017. "How Did Johnny Depp Find Himself in a Financial Crisis?" https://www.vanityfair.com/style/2017/07/johnny-depp-financial-crisis-money
[3] The Walmart Digital Museum. "Sam's Truck." https://www.walmartmuseum.com/content/walmartmuseum/en_us/timeline/decades/1970/artifact/2580.html

Take a client who loves fishing and having a boat. That is an expensive hobby, but I support that expense because it brings them happiness. But let's be clear: buying a boat to go fishing is not an investment. Boats are expensive with many underlying costs you don't necessarily consider until you actually own a boat. There is storage over the winter, inevitable repairs to be done, dock fees, gas costs, etc. But if your passion is fishing, if that's what you really enjoy doing and it's bringing you happiness, then I want to see you doing it.

I encourage my clients to have an "extras budget" for more frivolous things. This does not necessarily need to be a separate account–although that works well for some people–but rather, it's an attitude of making sure you're budgeting funds toward enjoying life. Transitioning from the accumulation years, in which you were focused on saving, to the distribution years, can be quite the adjustment. While a penny saved is a penny earned, you can't take your money with you to the grave. Don't deny yourself life experiences for fear that you should be investing that money instead to maximize long-term returns.

If you're always sacrificing for tomorrow, it is very difficult to be engaged with your finances because the money is not necessarily providing satisfaction. Planning for tomorrow, for your retirement, taking care of your family, and having enough money to protect yourself, are all very important things. But what are you working so hard for if you never enjoy the fruits of your labor? If, for you, that means having a nice car or boat, then that's what you should have as part of your "frivolous" budget. For me, I've always been happy spending money on traveling. When I'm traveling, I appreciate the memories I'm making with my family and the experiences we get to share together. That brings me the most happiness.

Of course, sometimes couples don't see eye to eye when they make financial plans together. Differing attitudes about money and how to spend or save can cause conflicts. Luckily for me, my wife, Erika, and I are both careful spenders. It's an attitude that was engrained in us during our upbringings. Erika comes from an upper-middle-class family, and her parents were not extravagant spenders. This passed down to her—she's a careful spender who loves getting a good deal. But we are probably the exception. It is much more common that one spouse is the saver and the other is the spender.

Couples that are more prone to financial conflicts might consider dividing their money into three categories: "yours, mine, and ours." The bulk of a couple's income goes into the "ours" category. These funds are used for shared living expenses, and can be saved toward shared financial goals. Then, some other portion of the income goes into "yours" and "mine." Each person has total discretion over how to spend that money, or whether to spend it all. For many couples, the best way to do that is to maintain separate bank accounts for discretionary spending. That way, if one person wants to buy a Rolex and the other person likes to go out with friends, they can both do that without creating a conflict or derailing their larger, shared financial goals.

Making Conscious Choices About Money

I'd like to impart one simple, essential lesson I learned early on that shaped my experience as an advisor: Even if you don't have a lot of money, it's still incredibly important to save. Both of my parents were teachers with relatively modest incomes. But since I was a little kid, my parents taught me to always save. 401(k)s and 403(b)s hadn't been around that long when they were working, but they put a little bit aside every month. My parents explained that you let the money sit and compound. They did not know a lot about investing, but they did teach me the importance of saving, and that was one of the earliest lessons I remember about money.

The important thing to remember about spending is that it isn't about budget categories or tax rates or return on investment. It really comes down to being conscious of your actions around money. A lot of people, probably the majority of people, spend whatever comes in. Obviously, that's not a good situation for the future. They're not investing, they're not protecting themselves, and they're not making conscious choices about how their immediate actions have long-term consequences.

Some people, especially young professionals, get discouraged when it comes to retirement saving. That's because they quickly learn that setting money aside for the future, means they have less to spend now. And they want to spend now! A simple way to alleviate that feeling is to have money automatically deducted from your paycheck and placed into your retirement account. The take-home pay will be a little less than you're used to having, but it won't be a huge difference. There is something psychologically different about having money set aside that you've never seen, versus taking money you've been given and having to set it aside yourself. In this case, "out of sight, out of mind" is a great mantra.

The second step in determining what to save versus spend, is to make sure you truly understand your fixed expenses. How much is your mortgage payment? What about your taxes, insurance, utilities, and all of that? What about healthcare? A child's tuition or sports expenses? Your average cost of groceries and gas? This calculation should be pretty straightforward. Once you understand those fixed costs, then the remainder of your income is used either for extra spending, saving, or a combination of the two. It's your choice how to categorize that money.

A lot of people think putting together a budget can be accomplished by going through a lengthy process of adding up everything that you spend month by month by month. For one thing, that's very difficult to do. Inevitably you miss things, so any budget that you get out of that exercise usually underestimates spending.

Some of my clients use Quicken or other similar software to track their spending. It gives a more accurate view of spending, but you must be willing to regularly update your spending data, make sure the category breakdowns are accurate, and so on. Some people enjoy digging around in their spending data, but for people who don't want to get into the weeds, there's a much easier way that I call, "Backwards Budgeting."

Here's how it works:

First, start with your take-home pay number. That figure is the amount that actually lands in your bank account. This is what you get after all the deductions are taken out of your paycheck, such as your 401(k) contribution, healthcare deduction, union dues, FICA, tax withholdings, and all those extra lines that show up on your pay stub. What you want is the bottom number–only the cash that comes into your bank account at the end of every pay period.

For a married couple, just to use easy numbers, let's say that's $10,000 net of taxes and everything else. Next, take a look at your bank account. What is the value of your bank account today? Let's say your balance there is $50,000.

So far, so good. Then go and look over your last year of account statements and make sure you didn't transfer any significant amount of cash out of that account for something other than spending, such as to another savings account or your emergency fund. In this example, let's say you didn't. So, you look at your statement from twelve months ago and see that you had $38,000 in the bank. This means you've saved $12,000 this year.

Naturally, that means you have saved $1,000 a month over the past year on average. That means out of take-home pay of $10,000, you're spending $9,000. If you need to save more, then you adjust your spending. That doesn't mean you need to track down every penny you've spent over the last year; just cut back on some of your larger spending categories.

Another approach that comes from behavioral finance experts is to simply automate the spending or saving for your goals. If you're saving $1,000 a month now but you want to start saving $1,500 a month, then you need to cut your spending down to $8,500 each month. You can automate a transfer of $1,500 every month to another savings account, investment account, or whatever. With $8,500 cash in your primary account every month, it is easier to stick to that spending goal because that is the available cash in the account. As long as you're saving for your priorities, paying your bills, and making steady progress on your financial goals, you don't necessarily need to spend time tracking and fretting about where your discretionary spending is going.

Of course, if you're piling up debt, you need to take a deeper dive into your spending to find expenses you can cut back on. It is critical to stop adding to debt, and to start paying down debt. You can do this by automating those payments, just like you do to achieve your other financial goals.

The Problem with Budgeting

The truth is that budgeting doesn't work very well in reality. People automatically do a better job of saving if they treat their monthly investments like a bill that comes due every month, whether that's saving through a 529 college plan or saving for a vacation. If you perceive saving as an obligation just like paying your mortgage or your taxes, then you will be disciplined and consistent about it.

Many disputes among couples crop up when it comes to how to allocate the household's income. Not only is this uncomfortable and difficult for both parties, but it can undermine your ability to make financial progress as a team. As previously mentioned, what helps a lot of couples struggling with these marital money issues, is to have most of the household income go into a joint account. Then each partner gets an individual pot of discretionary money to spend however they want, set aside in accounts of their own. This is particularly important in single income households, so each partner has some fun money of their own. Again, this is something you can handle with automatic transfers from the main bank account to the individual spending accounts.

The point of all this isn't to create a budget—I actually hate the word *budget*. It implies a limit on what you should be spending, overall and in different categories. It is more important to be *aware* of what you're spending now, so that you can get a realistic sense of what spending in retirement will look like. Then we can create a financial strategy that sets you up to be comfortable when you stop working.

Saving can be a huge motivator because you will see the benefit over time. Of course, this does not happen right away, especially with 401(k) accounts and other long-term savings. But when you start seeing that accumulation over time, you begin to appreciate it and gain a sense of accomplishment. Saving for retirement and saving for investing comes with a very slow sense of gratification, which is why a lot of younger people don't do it. Especially in our society today, everything's all about immediate gratification. It takes patience and discipline to reap the rewards of saving and investing.

Broadening Your Perspectives

One of the reasons to work with a financial professional is that it is very difficult to see the big picture of your financial life and how everything works together. Developing a broader perspective of how to realize financial goals is not a skillset most people understand.

There are many individual choices to make in order to achieve what you want in life, and how your money will play a role. As an advisor, I don't tell people what to do, but I help them see how all their choices work together.

Let's say someone asks me, "Can I afford a cottage up north?" This isn't an unusual question in Michigan, where people really love getting away on summer weekends to be near one of our lakes. I start by looking at how much they'll need for the down payment on that cottage, then the monthly mortgage payments, and all the additional expenses on top of that: property taxes, insurance, utilities, HOA fees, etc. Then I can put that into an income analysis and, based on all those factors, I can say: here's how much money you'll have and how long your money will last if you buy the cottage at your current savings rate, compared with what you'll have and how long your money will last if you pay for the cottage with a different rate of savings.

Once we're looking at that, we can see how that purchase translates to how many more years you'll need to work in order to make your money last until the age of ninety, or ninety-five, or whatever number you'd like to consider. When people start seeing those numbers, they get more clarify on big decisions. They can decide if they want to work longer, if they want to retire now, if they should scale down their lifestyle in retirement, if they should consider moving somewhere less expensive, or if they need to postpone buying the cottage for a while.

This type of analysis is very difficult for someone to do on their own. In additional to years of experience, you need an advisor with complex, sophisticated software to analyze these interwoven details. What happens if you want to retire at sixty-two with no cottage, versus buying the cottage and retiring at sixty-seven? You can leverage the advisor's expertise and complex software systems to make better, more informed decisions.

Most people make big financial decisions by shooting from the hip. They see there's extra money coming in, or there's extra money sitting on the sidelines, and they take a leap of faith by purchasing the cottage or other big-ticket item. They might even justify the purchase by saying, "I can always sell it if it doesn't work out." And that's true, but we all know the risk of taking a loss on the item. With a property, housing market risks are high. In addition to the normal fluctuations of property values, you would also take a loss on the sunk costs like closing costs, taxes, and all the other expenses that go into owning a second (or third or fourth) home.

While software should always be taken with a grain of salt, it is absolutely a useful tool in illustrating overall concepts and comparing the outcome of one scenario to another. In addition to illustrating the previous example of retiring at sixty-two without buying the cottage, versus buying the cottage and retiring at sixty-seven, we can also look at investment return scenarios during that time. What happens if the stock market is down ten-percent that year, or if the stock market is up six-percent another year? By evaluating various scenarios, people can make more informed decisions that make them feel comfortable.

Another advantage of looking at your entire financial picture is that there can be many angles to consider with a major purchase, and a misstep can end up being very expensive. After all, even if you're making an "extras" purchase, you still don't want to pay more than necessary.

Take the case of two of my long-time clients, who wanted to purchase the cottage up north that had been in their family for decades. The wife's father wanted to sell the cottage because he had health problems. He wanted to use proceeds to contribute to his grandchildren's education. My clients, who didn't have children, wanted to keep the cottage in the family and were ready to take out a second-home mortgage to buy the cottage. But that would've been a huge mistake.

Because of how property taxes are assessed in Michigan, purchasing the property from her father would have been a bad financial decision. That's because Michigan property tax increases are capped each year, regardless of any actual increase in property value. This is a significant advantage in vacation areas that largely depend on property taxes to support local government operations. When a property is sold, that property tax cap no longer applies; it gets reset with the new owner. Had my clients purchased the family cottage, the property taxes would have skyrocketed.

Furthermore, if my clients inherit the property later, they will get a step-up in basis. In other words, if the family decides to sell the cottage later, they would only be taxed on the increase in value between the time they inherited the cottage and when they sold, not on the increase that happened during her father's lifetime. Again, that can be a sizeable amount of money, especially in a popular vacation town.

Instead of buying the property outright, we arranged to leave the cottage in her father's name with my client as the beneficiary of the property. Then my clients gifted him cash annually until he'd been gifted the cottage's fair market value. Under current 2023 tax law, you're allowed to gift up to $17,000 a year to any one person without being subject to gifting taxes. Because this can be a strategy to dodge estate and income taxes, the government sets a limit on how much cash can change hands tax-free. Because my client is part of a married couple filing a joint tax return, she and her husband could each gift $17,000 to her father, for an annual total of $34,000 free and clear of tax consequence. Had her mother still been living and married to her father, that figure would double to $68,000, where my client and her husband could each gift $17,000 to her mother and another $17,000 each to her father. No mortgage, no interest, no real estate taxes or transfer fees, and, best of all, no change in the taxable value or tax basis of the cottage. Altogether, utilizing this approach helped my clients avoid tens of thousands of dollars in fees and taxes.

Considering Luxuries & Emotional Investments

Another consideration before plunging into your "extras" budget is that, beyond a financial commitment, big luxury purchases such as a cottage or a boat also come with time commitments. Cottages must be cleaned, opened up in the spring, and winterized and protected in the winter. Each trip involves a lengthy drive, grocery shopping, and turning on and off the gas, water, and security system. Having an expensive boat tied up at the dock demands that you gas it up, stock the coolers, and head out on the lake whenever there's a sunny weekend. With a boat, you'll also need to arrange for winterizing in the fall, winter storage and cleaning, tune-ups, and launching the vessel every spring. Even a membership to a country club or athletic club can begin to feel burdensome, especially when you're required to spend minimum amounts in the dining room and other facilities.

All of that can end up creating an obligation that turns a well-intentioned investment in family fun into a troublesome burden. You may feel like you're not getting value out of your boat, cottage, or club unless you're constantly using it. What this does is diminish the value of your investment, which was supposed to bring you joy but now is dragging you down. If that's how you feel, the right decision is probably to sell the cottage, get rid of the boat, or resign from the club. But many times, people balk. They think that because they've already spent a large amount of money into the purchase, maintenance, or dues, they "have to get their money" out of the purchase.

That's simply wrong. The idea to keep in mind in that situation is the concept of "sunk costs." Simply put, it means that once you've spent an amount of money, that money is gone for good. The cottage or boat, for example, is only worth what you can get when you sell it. You'll often see people overprice a home, for example, because they add up their purchase price, mortgage payments, and the cost of all their improvements. Then the house doesn't sell because even though the owner insists that "it's worth $400,000," the market values the home at $325,000.

The problem is that people get emotional about certain financial decisions and don't want to admit that they've lost money. But the market–whether that's for boats, cottages, stocks, or antiques–doesn't care what you paid or whether you've lost money. In fact, what you paid is irrelevant to the next buyer. And it really should be irrelevant to you, too. If something's not working for you, it's time to cut your losses and get rid of it. It doesn't make sense to keep making payments and spending money on upkeep and repairs for a boat or cottage you no longer enjoy, or to keep sending in dues checks and eating at a country club that's no longer fun. You'll end up continuing to spend money on something you really don't like and, if you're honest with yourself, that you don't even want anymore.

Another mistake people make when elevating their lifestyle is that they start confusing hobbies/personal enthusiasms with investments. If your passion is classic cars, for example, buying, restoring, and showing vintage Mustangs, Camaros, and GTOs is something you absolutely should do, as long as you can afford it and understand how the expenses will affect your overall financial plan. While it's certainly possible that those cars will appreciate in value, it doesn't make sense to start thinking about this portfolio of vintage cars as a prudent, long-term investing strategy.

Take the case of two clients who both are really into art photography. They've spent a lot of money over the years acquiring a beautiful collection of prints, to the point where they told me they need to stop because they've literally run out of room on the walls in their house. But if those pictures really and truly are going to work as an investment, then they need to be constantly monitoring the art photography market, identifying which specific photographers are becoming more popular with buyers, which ones are falling, and set specific goals for returns. Then, when a particular piece increases in value, they need to sell it off and realize the profit. What I've found, instead, is that most people rarely ever use their art as an investment. They are just buying art and justifying the cost by saying that it will increase in value eventually.

What tends to happen is that they're too busy and end up accumulating so much art, they don't even know where to put it. Think about how people can become emotionally connected to their stock purchases, maybe because they just really like the company or a parent used to work for that company and bought the stock for them. It can be difficult to make rational decisions about when to hold or sell that stock. This challenge is heightened even more with "alternative investments" like antiques or classic cars. There is often a stronger emotional attachment to these tangible items. At some point, however, the purchasing needs to get reined in, not just for the sake of your spending, but to relieve your kids of having to liquidate all this stuff when you're no longer around. Otherwise, you'll never sell at the right time and then, ultimately, your kids will end up selling the stuff without consideration and appreciation for market trends, because they don't know what they're doing. I can't tell you how many times I've seen kids sell off their parents' valuable possessions because they don't know the true value, and they just want to get rid of the stuff and be done with the hassle.

This kind of emotional attachment to an investment is easier to see with art or other items that you've personally selected, but I see the same considerations come into more standard kinds of investments, such as stocks. Someone may have a lot of company stock and feel loyal to the company, especially if they helped launch the operation or had a top leadership position there. They feel almost like it's a betrayal to start liquidating shares and balance their investments. This can also be true when people inherit stocks or other investments from a parent or spouse. They may feel a conflicting mix of nostalgia and family ties that can cloud their judgement and prevent them from making informed decisions. Some investors feel an attachment simply based on having personally selected that individual stock, and they don't want to "give up" on a company or admit that they made a mistake or have been hanging on to an underperforming investment for too long.

Whether it's art, grandpa's cottage, your collection of Fabergé eggs, or shares in the company that made you financially successful, it's important to separate your emotions from making rational decisions about your financial future. While this attachment is understandable, it can stand in the way of creating a quality portfolio. One of the best reasons for working with a financial planner you trust, is to get their objective, third-party perspective and prevent you from making financial decisions based on emotion. The advisor should want to do what's best for you going forward, rather than driving ahead while looking in the rearview mirror.

The Big Picture

The overarching theme behind any good financial advisor, is they should be doing so much more than just managing your investments. My skillset is above and beyond just picking stocks or bonds or finding the right fund. Remember, what's more important to your returns is the overall strategy you and your advisor create. Only a small amount of your investment returns come from specific stock selections, and an even smaller piece of your returns are the result of timing. The rest are all produced by asset allocation–the mix of what comprises your overall portfolio, how those investments work together, how they offset each other, and how they fit together in a total, comprehensive strategy that meets your needs. If you're just looking for a stock-picker, you don't need a true financial advisor.

The big advantage of looking at how factors like spending, saving, lifestyle choices, etc., come together in your life, is that you can then create a financial plan that reflects those same priorities. When the stock market starts fluctuating, whether it's about the election or Brexit or hurricanes or war or whatever, my clients do not frantically call me asking, "What do we do!?" We already factored market volatility into their plans, so they know they can withstand the storm. That peace of mind comes from knowing that you have direction and that we are allowing for some volatility in the market within the plan. When you do financial planning this way, people can be really comfortable and they stop worrying about their money, which is ultimately what people want.

CHAPTER 4

Retirement is About More than Money

Retirement lasting thirty years or longer means you'll have a lot of time on your hands when you retire. That means retirement planning is more than simply stashing away enough money to leave the workforce. It's also about deciding how you'll spend your post-work time. For some people, that means a second or part-time career, or pursuing your passions, whether that's charity work, community activism, or a hobby. You'll also want to factor in where you want to live, and whether your spouse wants to retire on your schedule, too.

All these decisions ultimately affect your financial plans for retirement. After all, if you really like golfing and want to golf as much as possible in retirement, your financial plan needs to support the costs associated with that hobby. That's why retirement planning is really life planning.

Do I WANT to Stop Working?

Another assumption people typically make is that they actually want to fully retire. The reality is, many people don't want to completely stop working; they just want to slow down and free up more time for the things they enjoy. I have one client in the auto industry who was offered a retirement buyout package, which he took but then immediately got a new job with a different company in the same industry. He is seventy-one years old, but wants to keep working and keep his brain active.

The goal is not to stop working for many people, because they like the challenge and the social interaction of work. Retirement needs to take social factors into account. When you're used to a busy office environment with lots of people, it can be shocking and lonely to suddenly not have that. Remember that financial well-being does not guarantee a healthy retirement. I advise people to think about what makes them passionate, then find a way to use that passion to pursue a hobby, part-time job, or volunteer work.

My mother was an English teacher and a librarian. She loves to read, and she's been a member of several book clubs where she interacts with people and discusses books, which is what she enjoys doing.

I have several clients with special needs kids. One became very active with a community organization that supports the same special needs as her kid. Another client enjoys helping underprivileged children find psychological help, and she can pursue that more in retirement. Another client has fostered handicapped dogs for years and now has time to volunteer at an animal shelter. There are all sorts of activities and opportunities available in the community. Retirement doesn't have to mean just golf and rocking chairs.

You can retire from work and leave your regular day-to-day job to create what I call a "slow retirement," where you're working part-time as an employee or consultant, or you're doing volunteer work. You're not working as much, but you're still actively involved in something that keeps you sharp, engaged, and challenged. That works very well for many people, but it works best if it's planned in advance, before you're reading to leave work. Perhaps you want to get specialized training, research an alternative or part-time career, or identify charities or organizations where you want to get involved. You can start that process well ahead of the day you turn in your resignation paperwork. This helps to more clearly refine your retirement plan.

I have an aunt in South Carolina. Every February, March, and April she does taxes for people who can't afford professional tax preparers. She's good with numbers, has always done that kind of work, and now it's her volunteer work. She enjoys it for a couple months out of the year and gets to set her own schedule.

Retirement Lifestyle

Pure and simple, strategizing and visualizing how you want to spend your retirement years, makes it much more likely those intentions will be realized. Most people think they'll just figure it out when the time comes. The reality is that most people don't sit down and think about how they really want to live their retirement years until they're already retired, and that can be a huge mistake.

I've actually seen many people retire, then unretire. This seems to happen most often when the person did not prepare for how to spend their time in advance. Without that plan, a lack of mental stimulation ensues. Imagine having a demanding job where you're very successful. You're constantly on the go, meeting deadlines, overseeing projects. You receive gratification and a sense of achievement from the work you do. And then you retire. You quickly realize you no longer have that sense of accomplishment. Furthermore, you realize you may never feel that same sense of satisfaction again. Without thinking through how to spend time in retirement, you never came up with a plan. If you don't have hobbies, maybe returning to work truly is your best bet. There's nothing wrong with getting that sense of fulfillment from work. I can relate; helping people every day and working with numbers is very fulfilling for me.

Sitting down and thinking deeply about how you want to spend your time in retirement is critically important. You don't want to be one of those people who must unretire, or someone who sits on the couch all day. Visualizing your dream retirement can be exciting. But it can also help you to become more proactive. After all, without the funds, that dream retirement will remain just that: a dream. The process of planning a retirement lifestyle can be a great motivator to ensure you're taking the necessary steps and following your savings goals and strategies. Are you saving enough? Are you doing it the optimal way? By visualizing the end result of a prosperous retirement, you will concentrate harder on making sure these questions are answered so that your dream can become your reality.

Start by considering how and where you'll spend your time. Do you want to travel, spend your days on the links of a golf-course community, spend time with your grandchildren, or downsize to a simpler, more maintenance-free life in a condominium or retirement community? One way to focus your thinking is to consider your bucket list items: what activities do you want to do; where do you want to travel; how do you want to establish your legacy. Make a list of your "must-do" items.

In addition to looking at the details, costs, and logistics of your plans, you also need to discuss your retirement ideas with your spouse. In many cases, one spouse wants to retire earlier or later than the other. Or one wants to fully retire while the other spouse wants to change careers, work part-time, or volunteer.

One idea that has worked well for many people is the concept of taking a "practice retirement" to test-drive your plans and assumptions. Make sure your retirement budget works and that you enjoy retirement as much as you predicted. If you can, take a few weeks of vacation time to spend in the place you want to live, doing the things you desire, and see how it all feels in person. Remember to ask yourself what this will feel like after the "honeymoon" period of retirement wears off. Will you still enjoy this routine six months from now, a year from now, five years from now? Then you can make adjustments to your plan accordingly.

Another lifestyle issue to consider is how you'll stay connected to friends, family, and your community—especially if you're planning to retire to a new locale. For many career-driven, high-achieving individuals, retirement can bring a sense of isolation following the loss of social networks, friends, and the accomplishments and sense of purpose that flows from working life and its well-established routine. According to the Institute of Economic Affairs in London, the chance that someone will suffer from clinical depression goes up 40 percent in retirement.[4]

So, in addition to making sure your retirement home is near the beach or convenient shopping, realize that you'll also need to take time and effort to establish new relationships and maintain existing ones. If you move into a new community, look to religious groups, clubs, social interest groups, etc., to create new networks, and plan on how you'll set times and activities to get together with old friends instead of waiting for an invitation.

---

[4] Daniel Kurt. Investopedia. December 28, 2020. "How To Combat Depression After Retirement."
https://www.investopedia.com/articles/retirement/120516/retirement-and-depression-6-ways-overcome-it.asp#citation-1

Time in Retirement

You can also think about creating a "retirement schedule" of exercise and socialization, which can ward off depression, improve your health, and create a sense of overall well-being. You can also consider ways to keep your mind active by volunteering or going back to school, whether that's learning about entertaining subjects in continuing education classes, private instruction to learn an instrument or skill, or pursuing classes on a topic you've always wanted to master.

Beyond money and investing, retirement planning comes down to how you want to live your life and occupy your time. What are you passionate about? What's interesting to you? Those are the things that are really important. If you love to travel, traveling should be at the top of your priority list. But it also needs to be budgeted for. If you really like golf, make sure to play as much as your body will allow. However, golf is a fairly expensive hobby, so take that into account if you plan to golf every day or multiple times a week. Once you decide how you'd like to spend your time in retirement, you can figure out what your expenses will be, and you can begin to gain some clarity on retirement.

I have clients run through a checklist of, "What are the things you want to address?" This exercise helps them identify what is important to them, and it helps me establish a framework for helping them toward those goals. Most people will eventually retire, but what if you want to sell a home, make home improvements, or buy a new or second home? Your parents' declining health could be an issue. Maybe you want to help your children or grandchildren with their education expenses. Do your plans change if you receive an inheritance from a parent?

Those considerations all are part of the retirement planning process, but people usually don't think carefully about them—if at all—until we start that conversation. The earlier you can envision your retirement, the more clarity you gain and the better prepared you will be for retirement.

Unretiring

If you retire simply because you qualify for Social Security or your pension kicks in, you might be completely bored before you know it and wanting to return to the workforce. You may have figured out your financial situation in retirement based on not working, but now you're back to work and generating some income again. This can change all of your tax assumptions.

One of the biggest issues that comes up in "unretirement" is Social Security benefits. There was once a time when you could collect Social Security, then reverse it, pay it back, and continue to delay collecting. This was useful if you return to work unexpectedly, and want to continue deferring your Social Security because you're generating wages again. While this feature is still available, it is limited to only the first year you collect Social Security, along with several other requirements. If you make a mistake and figure it out early on, there's a bit of an escape clause. But it's better to have a well-considered strategy and aim to get the timing of collecting benefits right from the start.

The same sort of thing can happen with your pension, too. Some of my clients retired early from good jobs with the Big Three Detroit automakers. They worked for their employer for thirty years, so they retired in their mid- to late-fifties and started collecting their pensions. Once you turn on your pension, you cannot reverse that decision. Once it's done, it's done. In some cases, it is better to defer the pension rather than taking it early.

Age and the Workplace

Another issue that comes up fairly often is how many people retire earlier than they intended. This can be due to many reasons, but most commonly, health problems make it too hard for aging people to work. Corporate downsizing can also be the culprit, and what demographic is usually the first target of downsizing? It is generally the more senior employees with the fatter paychecks and more expensive benefits packages. We all know that ageism occurs in the workforce; it is cheaper to get rid of the older employees and hire in the "young gun" who will work for less money and fewer benefits.

And how easy is it to find a new job at the age of sixty? We all know the answer to that question. You're either too experienced, too expensive, or too close to retirement age.

Another common situation is feeling left behind and overlooked because younger colleagues are armed with the latest technology and techniques, whereas your area of expertise may now be dated or becoming obsolete. This is especially common in the IT/technology field. It can feel like the new, younger workforce is taking over and you're no longer part of the team. This can have a negative impact on morale; then the work suffers and becomes less fun. So even if you aren't forced out, it can feel that way.

In other industries that don't require much innovation, it could be the *lack* of change that becomes the issue. We have clients in banking, or clients who work as CPAs for large corporations, who have mentioned this problem. Sure, the forms change each year, but ultimately, it is the same job over and over for thirty years. And because they are working for big corporations, there isn't the gratification of seeing how their results benefit real people. So over time, they become less and less engaged. Their work becomes boring or dissatisfying after so many years, and they really want to leave work or, in some cases, are forced to leave because their dissatisfaction becomes apparent.

The reality is that people often anticipate working until sixty-five, then retiring just after their sixty-fifth birthday. That's the most common age people anticipate retiring, but it does not happen that way very often. The reality is that people need to plan on retiring earlier than they expect. Just look at these numbers from the Employee Benefit Research Institute to understand why:

- 12 percent of workers plan to retire before age sixty, but the actual number is 31 percent;
- 22 percent of workers plan to retire between the ages of sixty and sixty-four, but in practice, it's 38 percent of workers;
- 24 percent of workers plan to retire at sixty-five, but only 11 percent of people work long enough to retire at that age;
- 12 percent of workers plan to retire when they're between sixty-six and sixty-nine, and 14 percent do;
- 29 percent plan to retire at age seventy or older (or never retire at all), but only 7 percent achieve that; and

- 65 percent of workers expect to retire at age 65 or later, but 69 percent of workers retired *before* hitting age 65.[5]

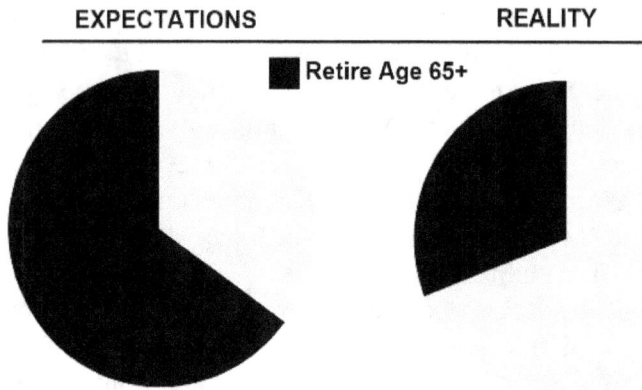

The issue with retiring earlier than planned, is that it sabotages your financial goals in a few ways. First, your retirement savings now has to start supporting you for a longer amount of time, which reduces how much you can withdraw each year. Second, you start pulling your money out early, which reduces the potential for growth in your investments. And third, you lose time when you would have been earning income and making additions to your retirement accounts. You may also be forced into taking Social Security or a pension early, which further reduces your monthly income in retirement.

Slow Retirement and Retiring Earlier

If you're retiring because you lost your job, were forced out, or became dissatisfied with work, I suggest looking for ways to rejuvenate your career with less focus on corporate success and more focus on your happiness.

I've met many people who transition to a different role via a "slow retirement." Instead of leaving work outright, you may be able to work for your current employer as an independent contractor or

---

[5] Employee Benefit Research Institute. 2022. "2022 Retirement Confidence Survey." https://www.ebri.org/docs/default-source/rcs/2022-rcs/2022-rcs-summary-report.pdf?sfvrsn=a7cb3b2f_12

consultant. Or you could work on a consultancy basis in a similar role with another company that would value your years of experience.

This arrangement can be rejuvenating. It's a new and exciting challenge. You typically have more control over your hours and working conditions, who you work with, and what type of assignments you accept. Your experience and knowledge are something you can take with you without having to go out and find another permanent, full-time position, especially in industries where companies may not be open to hiring older workers in the first place. Besides, your employer might actually love this consultancy arrangement. They get to move you off their books. No more benefits to pay. No more pension accrual (one of their favorite things!), and no long-term commitment to your salary. This can be a win-win for both sides.

For example, one of my clients was an engineer who worked for Ford. When he retired, he started working for their performance division. He goes out to their Proving Grounds and does testing of new vehicles, driving around in vehicles that aren't even in production yet. He has a great time doing it, and he can do it part-time. He's creating his own schedule and is really enjoying himself. He only planned to do this for a couple of years, but it's been over five years now and he wants to continue doing this work as long as possible.

It's quite shocking how often my clients move up their retirement dates. When I originally meet with them, they tell me their plan is to retire at a certain age, but really there was no rhyme or reason to selecting that particular retirement age. It was essentially picked out of thin air. However, once we begin the process of putting a financial plan together, they start to realize how the numbers shake out both before and after retirement. Then reasonable assumptions can be made about what a realistic retirement age might be.

Many people have done a great job of saving, but they have no idea what that actually means for them. They just have a bunch of investment accounts. So when they see a plan that demonstrates how to properly use that money to retire at a desired date, they think, 'I did a better job than I thought!' It's a great feeling to show folks a retirement plan that is so impactful, that they decide to retire earlier and spend more time doing the things they really enjoy.

Sometimes this realization can backfire. Once a person realizes they no longer have to work, they might start finding faults in their workplace. This can serve as an excuse to pull the trigger to retire earlier.

One of my clients comes to mind. He told me initially that he planned to retire at age sixty-seven. But he had a big pension available at age sixty-two, so I suggested retiring at that age. Then his tune changed. He started to focus more on problems at work and became generally dissatisfied with working there. He said, "I want to retire NOW!" But he wasn't sixty-two yet. I had to remind him that his ability to retire earlier than originally planned was contingent upon the pension. Without the pension, he would have to take large amounts from his portfolio to support his lifestyle. He was jumping the gun and getting overly exciting about the idea of retiring, but he still needed to stick out those last few years at that employer.

It's amazing to see the power that professionals in my industry can have in developing a client's future. There is a huge opportunity to help people live that dream retirement. One of the biggest steps in doing this is simply seeing the plan. It is pretty common when people come to see me, they have no idea or concept of what they have and how those assets would all fit together. But illustrating visually how the puzzle pieces should be arranged provides reassurance that they've done a good job of saving. And suddenly they realize they will have a comfortable, worry-free retirement. Witnessing this realization and the sudden shift in a person's attitudes about retirement, knowing that I have played a major role in bringing their retirement dreams to light, is one of my life's greatest satisfactions.

Lifestyle, Spending, and Taxes

The assumption, especially with tax-deferred retirement accounts such as IRAs and 401(k)s, is that you will be in a lower tax bracket when you retire. The idea is that by being in a lower tax bracket in the future, you can let these accounts grow tax-free and pay income tax on the withdrawals later on at a lower tax rate. It sounds great in theory, but if you've been a good saver, many times it's unlikely that you'll move into a lower tax bracket in retirement. Now, if you haven't saved much and you're planning to live off Social Security and dramatically reduce your lifestyle in retirement, then yes, you will probably drop into a lower tax bracket. But most people I meet with have been good savers and are not interested in making a drastic reduction in their lifestyle. In fact, what I find most frequently is that many people actually see their tax bracket increase in retirement.

If you've been good at saving and investing in a tax-deferred account, you've got a healthy nest egg built up. For most people, once you hit the age of seventy-two, or up to age seventy-five depending on when you were born, the IRS requires you to start taking a minimum withdrawal called a *required minimum distribution* (RMD). This is the government's way of saying, "It's time to pay taxes on that money." That money has built up tax-free over the years, but it can't continue forever. Once you hit your RMD age, which is currently somewhere between the ages of seventy-two and seventy-five, depending on your birth year, you will be required to take out an increasing percentage of your tax-deferred accounts every year, and these distributions are taxed at current income tax rates. When combined with your other sources of income, that required distribution can easily push you into a higher tax bracket.

Let's say you saved one-millions dollars in your tax-deferred IRAs and 401(k)s. At age seventy-two or so, your RMD is about $35,000. Let's say your spouse did the same. Now your household income is $70,000. Perhaps you each earn an average of $2,800 per month from Social Security. That's another $67,000 in annual income. Just from those two sources alone, you're now up to $137,000 in taxable income. If you have a pension or other investment income, that income climbs even higher. And this is assuming that you're only taking the *minimum* from your retirement accounts. All of this income is taxed at normal income tax rates. Many people filing their first tax return in retirement are shocked at how much money they earned, and realize that what they've learned about putting money away in tax-deferred accounts is not all it's cracked up to be.

Additionally, people's tax deductions tend to disappear in retirement. A common tax deduction is 401(k) contributions, but that stops when you retire. Many people pay off their mortgage before retirement, so they lose the mortgage deduction. Monetary charitable contributions often decline because rather than writing a check to their favorite charity, many retirees would rather volunteer their time to the charity. So their charitable contribution becomes TIME more so than money.

The problem is compounded if tax rates rise in the future, and this is currently guaranteed to happen. The tax "discounts" put in place in 2018 are scheduled to return to pre-2018 levels in 2026. This is a scheduled tax increase that is guaranteed to happen unless current tax law is changed between now and January 2026.

The tax rates that we pay now in 2023 are historically some of the lowest tax rates the United States government has ever enforced.

The highest tax bracket is currently 37-percent. This will return to pre-2018 levels of 39.6-percent in 2026. But back in 1944, after World War II, the highest tax bracket was 94-percent. The highest tax bracket stayed over 70-percent for the next three decades, through the 1970s. So, the government is certainly capable of raising income tax rates to very high levels and has already set the precedent of doing so. Even if we never see 70-percent tax rates again, the risk of tax rates increasing at some point in the future seems a sure thing considering existing levels of national debt and government spending.

These are reasons why I stress diversifying your retirement assets for taxes as well as investments. Once you get into retirement, your focus goes from accumulating money to preserving it, while leaving you enough room for withdrawals to live on. Taking a savvy approach of saving in different "tax buckets" leaves you with many more potential strategies to take advantage of and reduce your overall tax burden.

Besides the issue of taxes, you also need to consider the real effects of inflation on your living expenses going forward. While inflation can be a corrosive and real danger to your retirement, it can also be misconstrued as a scare tactic. If you visit online retirement calculators at the big mutual fund companies' websites, they often estimate that a typical person needs several million dollars to pay for their retirement. The reason for such a high figure, is that these calculators use a 3-percent estimate for inflation. So, if all your expenses increase by 3-percent every year, your expenses are going from $80,000 a year to more than $150,000 a year—nearly doubling—in a twenty-year period.

But let me ask you this: Do people really spend 3-percent more on everything every year? Not really. If you have a mortgage, your mortgage doesn't increase by 3-percent a year. Your taxes might, food and energy might. But, most importantly, I find that people don't change their spending habits that much over time. People become a little bit more frugal as they get older because things just LOOK more expensive, so they don't want to buy as much as they once did. They're so used to remembering the day when gas was $1.29 a gallon and now you have to pay $4.30 and it looks ridiculous. Movies have been a few bucks for most of your life. Are you now going to spend $15 to go to the movies and buy a $6 popcorn? For a lot of people, I see that the answer is "no." I see that even people who've been spenders their whole life, cut back a little bit in retirement.

People find alternatives. When you used to be able to pay three-dollars for a movie, you're not going to pay $15, and you start renting movies or end up with Netflix or getting DVDs from the library. You start looking for alternatives that are a little bit cheaper, whether you realize it or not.

There is also that fact that people tend to slow down as they get older. As you age, many of the more costly activities that you once enjoyed become less fun, simply because your body can't keep up any more. You won't be taking ski vacations anymore when your knees hurt or your back aches. Your days on the golf course may become a thing of the past after hip problems develop. Spending in retirement changes over time due to what I call, the Phases of Retirement.

The Phases of Retirement

At the very beginning of retirement, we often see a spike in spending during what planners call the honeymoon phase. This is when you're excited about being retired and you want to go on more trips than usual, do more golfing, or whatever your hobby may be. After a lifetime of working, newly retired people want to cram in all the fun activities they never had time to do while working. You know that bucket list you've been adding to for years? Now you finally have the time to tackle it! How long that honeymoon period lasts varies for people; sometimes it's two months, sometimes it's six months, sometimes it's two years.

However long the honeymoon phase of retirement lasts for you, it will probably be the shortest part of your overall retirement timeline. Overall, your retirement is going to go through a few different periods—what I call the "go-go years," then the "slow-go years," and then the "no-go years."

When you're younger and healthy, you travel more, you become more active in your hobbies, or you pursue new activities. As you age, you gradually slow down over time or even stop doing a lot of those things. Your knees might hurt, or you're not as inspired—after all, how many times do you need to see the Grand Canyon? It's tiring to travel, you're getting on and off planes, you may not know the language, and these challenges can be exhausting for people. These are your "slow-go years." You haven't totally stopped doing the things you enjoy, but you're not doing them as frequently anymore. You tend to gravitate towards staying at home and living your comfortable, non-working life.

Then comes the "no-go period" where you're mostly staying at home, you're not driving much anymore, and your schedule is free of activities and commitments. Life becomes pretty routine and nice. You get up, have your coffee in the morning, and read the paper. Your big event of the week may be going to the grocery store, running errands, or grabbing a bite to eat at a restaurant. That can be a nice, comfortable life. You don't have to be in a nursing home or assisted living facility for that to happen. You just kind of do your thing and enjoy life that way. It is a very common lifestyle in later retirement.

What all of this means is that your spending is not steady throughout your retirement years. At first, you'll be establishing your retirement lifestyle—moving, buying a boat, getting new golf clubs, etc.—and that's going to be as expensive, if not more expensive, than what you were spending in your last few years of working. Then you'll need less money as you slow down. Maybe your retirement home is paid off, you might be down to one car that's also paid off, and you're mostly focused on keeping things status quo. Then, as you do less, you spend less.

CHAPTER 5

You're the One on the Hook

When it comes to retirement investing, there are three phases: Accumulation, Preservation/Income, and Distribution.

The Accumulation phase happens when you're younger and working. The focus is saving up money. You've got lots of time to make up any losses, and you can handle investment risk with no problem. The situation becomes very different when you get close to retirement. Everything changes within five years of retirement. That's when people realize they will need to use that money relatively soon, and they become more sensitive and emotional with swings in the market.

Many people are actually pretty good about putting money away and ignoring it, which is a good thing when you're in your thirties and forties. Just try to save money, don't worry about the market, and even if it goes down, you can actually cheer for a market to crater because then you get to buy more shares.

It's totally different when you get into your mid-fifties. Then you really need to start looking at your investments in a different way because your view on the market will change, whether you like it or not. You will become more emotional about downturns because you'll realize that you'll need that money sooner. You don't want it to be a situation where, when you're five years away from retirement, there's a big downturn that prompts you to think, "Oh no! I have to keep working longer because my portfolio value just plummeted!" Your attitude changes whether you recognize it or not.

Around age fifty-five or sixty is when people typically start to realize that they need to be more consistent, that their plan needs to be more comprehensive, and that they need to get help from a financial professional. Before that time, people take all kinds of different approaches to how they're saving and investing.

I recently met with someone who told me, "You know, I learned how to invest from my plumber, of all people." When he was younger, his plumber said, "See this box of tools I have here? Think of your investments like each one of these tools; you just keep throwing tools in the box, then close up the box, and don't think about it. That's what you should do: just keep accumulating, putting stuff in the box, and just let it sit there." That's fine advice for most people when they are trying to accumulate money in their earlier stages.

Whether or not you get financial advice from your plumber (or mechanic or doctor or landscaper), it also makes sense to get professional direction during the accumulation phase of your working life. No matter your stage of life, seeing a professional and getting guidance and direction can be very helpful. Sometimes people miss the simple stuff, such as realizing that they're contributing to their 401(k) account when they could be contributing to their Roth 401(k) instead.

The New Retirement

Pension plans are going the way of the dodo, leaving most Americans with do-it-yourself pensions. In 1975, the number of Americans covered by employer-paid pension plans was 33-million compared with less than 12-million people in plans where they saved money out of their own paychecks. By 2014, the number of workers covered by pension plans had barely budged to less than 38-million—but the number of workers saving in their own retirement accounts soared to nearly 95-million.[6]

---

[6] Employee Benefits Security Administration United States Department of Labor. September 2021. "Private Pension Plan Bulletin Historical Tables and Graphs 1975-2019."
https://www.dol.gov/sites/dolgov/files/ebsa/researchers/statistics/retirement-bulletins/private-pension-plan-bulletin-historical-tables-and-graphs.pdf

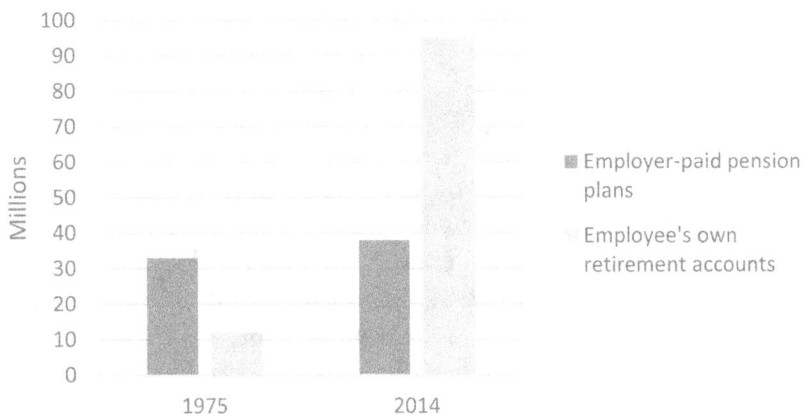

The New Retirement Structure

- Employer-paid pension plans
- Employee's own retirement accounts

The traditional approach to planning for retirement was the concept of a "three-legged stool": Social Security, pension, and savings. These three components would comprise the retirement income sources for many Americans. But now pensions are nearly unheard of for most Americans, leaving people with a two-legged stool that's guaranteed to collapse unless they build that missing pension leg for themselves.

Life spans have increased dramatically since pensions were more commonplace. As people are living longer, pensions need to pay out longer. This leaves companies paying out more money in pensions than they could have predicted decades ago. That's why so many companies now want you on the hook for coming up with your retirement money, not them. They can't afford to have you work for thirty years, and then financially support you in retirement for another thirty years. The numbers just don't work out. That's why most companies have embraced switching to defined contribution plans as opposed to defined benefit plans.

Another way that you're on the hook for your own retirement is the possibility that Social Security and Medicare benefits may be reduced someday in the future, and that employers will reduce pension benefits—such as healthcare coverage—in retirement. And, as I'll mention again shortly, there's always the risk that a pension plan may go into default and reduce your payment amount. That's the case for many City of Detroit pensioners, who saw their healthcare benefits completely eliminated and pension payouts reduced during after the city's 2013 bankruptcy. In some cases, retirees were forced to repay bonus payments that had been approved earlier by their pension administrators.

Pensions

If you're one of those people lucky enough to have received some kind of pension during your career, it's most likely been closed or frozen. If your plan is no longer active, your only decision is when to start collecting the pension, and whether to take it as a single annuity for your lifetime, or collect a smaller amount while living so your surviving spouse can continue receiving some benefit should you pass away first.

With some plans, workers stop accruing any new benefits once they've hit a certain age or specific number of years working with the company. At that point, it makes sense to start taking the pension as soon as the full payment is available. Your pension is a lifetime benefit (or more than a lifetime, if you're sharing the benefit with your spouse), so taking payments as soon as you're fully eligible doesn't affect your future monthly payouts—they'll still be the same. Even if you're still working and don't need the income, you can invest that money in your personal accounts. Yes, those payments will be considered taxable income, but you'll still come out ahead.

Deciding Whether to Take a Lump-Sum Payout

Pension decisions get more complicated if you're still in an active plan and receive a lump-sum buyout offer. This happens when the company wants to rid itself of the burden of managing pensions, clean up the books, and lock in its pension costs. Pensions are unlimited, lifetime benefits—if you live to be 110-years-old, you'll still be getting a monthly payment. If you take the survivorship option, then the pension payments continue until your surviving spouse dies.

Now consider that a lot of these pensions were implemented thirty or forty years ago, when people didn't spend thirty years in retirement, life spans were shorter, and medical treatments weren't nearly as advanced and effective. Your employer would rather nail down the cost of your pension by offering you a lump sum and getting all that risk off the books now. In some cases, the employer offers to purchase an annuity, which will belong to you and replace your pension payments with a monthly annuity payment. Either way, the employer's cost is guaranteed and the company's responsibility for your pension is done.

That makes sense for the company, but in a lot of cases taking a lump-sum payout makes a lot of sense for workers, too. I believe that if a properly invested lump sum can generate similar income to the pension payment, it's a good bet to take the money and drop your pension. Otherwise, you're going to bear the risk that the company might not be able to pay your pension. Now, pensions are insured by a government entity called the Pension Benefit Guarantee Corporation (PBGC), but that's no guarantee you'll receive your full pension, especially if you're a highly paid employee. If you're a sixty-year-old eligible for a single-employer pension plan that goes broke, the PBGC limits your monthly payment in 2024 to a maximum of $4,620.17 a month, or $55,442.04 per year.[7] But this is PBGC's *maximum*, not your pension plan's. For most pension plans that get paid out through PBGC, you'll never see anything close to the PBGC maximum. That's because the typical PBGC payout is 50-percent of your benefit. In order to get that $4,620.17 per month maximum from PBGC, your actual pension amount from your company would have been over $9,000 per month. If your company pension amount was supposed to be $5,000 per month, now you're getting around $2,500 per month from PBGC. If you were relying on the bigger number to sustain your retirement, you now have to figure out how to make do on half.

Although the choice to take or reject a buyout offer is very complex, in general, I favor taking the lump sum. There are so many factors to consider, and so many unknowns, including longevity. No one knows how long you will live. I might be a bit biased because my dad only collected three months of pension payments before he died, but that's a real-life illustration of just how unpredictable the entire question of retirement and longevity can be. Had my dad had a lump sum option, he could have collected the lump sum and passed it down

---

[7] Pension Benefit Guaranty Corporation. October 20, 2023. "Maximum Monthly Guarantee Tables." https://www.pbgc.gov/wr/benefits/guaranteed-benefits/maximum-guarantee

to me and my brother. Instead, he received three-months of payments, and then, that money was gone.

For most people, when they're given the option of taking a pension buy-out, it's either keep it with the company or take it as a lump sum. In those cases where the company offers the choice of taking a lump sum or allowing the company to move the pension to a fixed annuity, you can always take the lump sum, then buy your own annuity. In that situation, the choice comes down to whether your advisor can find a better annuity than the one offered by your employer. Even though the choice seems simple, there are a number of things to consider. One is the strength of the company—do you think your company will still be around in thirty years to make your payments? Remember, we used to have cameras that used film. Who would've thought that Kodak would become irrelevant? How comfortable are you if you have a pension from Sears these days?

With the lump sum offers, I am able to perform a series of calculations to determine the best mathematical decision. This process is rather complex to the average person, but not to someone like myself who runs these calculations all the time. For example, if your pension is offering you a thousand dollars a month versus a $200,000 lump sum, I can figure out the rate of return they're expecting if you live an average life expectancy. If you can get a 3.5-percent rate of return on the lump sum by investing it, you will usually outperform the company pension.

Most people like the idea of taking the lump sum, especially once I show people how we can replicate the pension payments, AND still have a death benefit value to pass on to your beneficiaries. I find the people who prefer the annuity payments have concerns over spending it all, so getting the income steadily over time works better for them, even if it's not necessarily the best financial decision.

Before I go any further, let me say that deciding between taking a pension or accepting a lump-sum buyout offer is a very complicated decision. It's going to depend on where you are in your work history, what your other retirement assets look like, your plan for when you'd like to retire, the financial condition of the company offering the buyout, what you plan to do with that money, and more, including the size of the buyout and your own investment strategy. While I do generally find that most people will be better off by taking the buyout, this is a decision that's best made by getting the advice of a trustworthy financial professional. Like nearly everything in financial planning, the "best" decision depends on each individual's situation.

Finding the Best Strategy

A big factor in the pension versus lump sum decision is looking at what provides the most safety, and weighing that against what produces the most money.

Here's an example: I've been working with a client who's been offered a good lump-sum buyout by one of Detroit's Big Three auto manufacturers. We all know that the automakers have been through a very challenging time in the last decade and came out in good shape—but the auto industry still faces a sprawling landscape of unknowns. Even now that General Motors Co. is profitable, for example, the company is making drastic adjustments to its workforce and structure because of uncertainty about the economy, electric vehicles, and other unknowns.

What I've proposed is that the client takes his lump sum and divides it among a few immediate annuities from several different insurance companies. These annuities would pay a monthly income for his lifetime, just like the pension. We can purchase immediate annuities from some very big, established, and financially secure insurance companies that would give my client a guaranteed payout over time that would be only $20 less than his monthly pension payout. Now, you might be thinking, "Why take this approach when it's less money than the pension payment?" Think of it like an insurance policy. For just $20 per month, we can get the money in the client's control as opposed to the employer. This eliminates the risk of any problems that could hit his automaker employer down the road and ultimately impact his pension.

Despite all that, he told me he's still considering staying with his company pension. I reminded him that if his employer goes under, the pension guarantee corporation probably won't cover his whole pension. With the annuities, he's guaranteed to get nearly the entire amount should the insurance company go under. But he's still confused. He told me, "Well, the chief financial officer of the company said that our pension is fully funded." Well, of course the CFO is going to say that. That's their job. And while it's true now, that doesn't mean the pension will be fully funded in the future. If the company goes bankrupt in the future, it does not matter that the pension is fully funded.

But, since pension plans are guaranteed by a government entity, why should you worry? As I mentioned earlier, right now the pension guarantee program is fully funded for single-payer plans, up to the legal benefit cap. If you were a high-earning employee whose payments would have been more than the limit, you'll lose the difference. There also are concerns that, if more pension plans are terminated or insolvent, that the guarantee corporation won't be able to pay 100-percent of benefits up to the limit anymore. This is another risk to consider.

If you're covered by a multi-payer pension—such as through a union that works with more than one company—your benefit payment could be reduced, according to a somewhat complex formula. And, as I noted earlier, the fund to guarantee those multi-employer pensions is grossly under-funded. If that situation worsens, nobody knows if Congress would add taxpayer money to the guarantee funds, which are financed through pension insurance premiums. Here's what the guarantee corporation says about multi-employer plans:

"PBGC's guarantee is based on a pension for each year of service a person earns under his or her pension plan. As a monthly benefit amount, we guarantee a payment equal to:
- 100% of the first $11 of the plan's monthly benefit rate, **plus** 75% of the next $33 of the monthly benefit rate,
- **times** the participant's years of credited service.

If the plan provides a benefit of more than $44 per month per year of service, the guarantee disregards that higher level.
- PBGC's maximum monthly guarantee, therefore, is $35.75 per month (($11 x 100%) + ($33 x 75%) = $35.75) times a participant's years of credited service.

The guaranteed benefit is not adjusted for inflation or cost-of-living increases."[8]

One way that I explain why I generally favor a lump sum payout is to ask clients to think about what they're doing when they choose the pension as opposed to a lump sum. They're effectively writing a

---

[8] PBGC Pension Benefit Guaranty Corporation. August 13, 2021. "Multiemployer Insurance Program Facts."
https://www.pbgc.gov/about/factsheets/page/multi-facts

check for whatever that lump sum amount is, to their former employer. If you have a $700,000 lump sum available and you choose to take the annuity, that's the equivalent of writing your employer a check for $700,000 to fund your pension.

People think, "I'll just keep things simple and stick with the pension." And that's certainly the easier choice. But if people stop to think instead of how they're essentially writing a check to their employer for many hundreds of thousands of dollars, I bet more people would say, "No, absolutely not. I don't want to do that." It's all about looking beyond the surface of the issue and thinking things through more in-depth.

Don't Put All Your Eggs in One Basket

Some people in retirement can become far too reliant on their former employers, such as when they own company stock along with a company pension and company-paid healthcare. Everything revolves around the strength of this one single company. If something happens to that company, you can have your pension cut, your health benefits cut, and the stock goes away. That's a huge potential problem. That's one risk I really try to emphasize to people: the size of your position in any one entity, including your employer or former employer, should not create a situation where you're severely negatively impacted if something bad happens to that company.

You shouldn't have more than 5-percent of your portfolio subject to any one company, and even that much still is a high percentage. People investing through their 401(k) accounts often make the mistake that workers did at Enron—they put a whole bunch of money in the company stock because it seems like it's doing well. But if that company runs into problems, you're in big trouble.

To be realistic, you have to realize that the company is not thinking about your family. You're just a shareholder, and it doesn't matter if you worked for the company or for another firm. People will often feel that they need to leave their money in company stock as a form of loyalty or commitment, which means emotion is the motivator. It's another form of emotional investing, just in a different way. It is important to put emotion aside and stick to common sense investing.

Pension Replacement

So if you take the lump sum, what do you do with it? The essence of this strategy is *pension replacement*. A traditional employer pension is a certain type of annuity, called an *immediate annuity*. You can buy a product that literally duplicates a pension—all you have to do is purchase an immediate annuity.

Now, buying this type of annuity is not ideal for most people. With an immediate annuity, just like with a company pension, you "use it or lose it" and the decision is irrevocable. I always ask people in this situation, "So you're going to write a $200,000 check to an insurance company and they're going to agree to pay you a set amount every month for the rest of your life no matter how long you live. But when you write that check, whether it's $200,000 or $2 million—poof!—that money is no longer yours; it belongs to the annuity company. If you die before receiving the amount you paid, you've lost money and there's nothing leftover for any heirs, other than your spouse if you had a spousal benefit on that annuity."

How excited would you be to write a check for that much money and immediately see it disappear?

Instead, what you should do is create an endowment for yourself. You do that through diversification, using a whole portfolio of different investments. This includes traditional stocks and bonds, but it also needs to include alternatives, such as commodities, real estate, and preferred stock. These are things that don't move in lock step with stocks and bonds. I also like including fixed and fixed index annuities within a portfolio to provide not only protection against market losses, but also to provide stability and a steady place to generate income. By developing this type of portfolio, we can almost always outperform the company's annuity payments, leave the rest to your spouse and/or heirs, and provide steady and reliable income.

The College Distraction

Not understanding or, even worse, ignoring the benefits of investing early and often, is the major culprit for most Americans' financial problems. The issue I see for many people is not that they bought *this* stock or *that* annuity or some insurance policy. It's that they simply haven't saved enough money. Because retirement feels very far off into the future, saving for retirement often takes a back seat to more immediate spending needs.

The most common scenario I see with this, is that once a couple has children, they put all their money toward bringing up the kids and putting them through school, saving for college and graduate school, and so on. Then, after the kids are in college, they realize, "OK, now I need to save for my retirement." But that's too late to leverage compounding over time, and it also gives their investments less time to recover if there's a recession or major market downturn.

Retirement savings and college savings should be happening in conjunction with one another, along with all your other financial priorities. You shouldn't be putting all your eggs into college savings and whatever the kids' activities are, at the expense of your own saving. If you want to live comfortably in retirement, you need to commit to saving specifically for retirement. Increase your 401(k) contributions, free up cash, and do whatever you can to create a bigger nest egg.

For a lot of people, it's very important to get their kids through college. But education is a big bill. People often put more emphasis on paying for their kids' college than saving for their own retirement. I've seen the circumstance too many times that college tuition bills become priority number one. This diverts too much of the parents' retirement money. They end up cannibalizing their retirement to pay for their kids. Parents need to be reminded that nobody's going to lend you money for your retirement expenses, but people will lend your kids money to get a college degree. You can borrow money for college, but you can't borrow money for retirement. You can apply for scholarships to help with college expenses; there are no scholarship programs for retirement.

Like retirement, there are a lot of myths and misconceptions about the cost of college, driven by the fact that, just like retirement projections, figuring out how much you'll need to save always produces an intimidatingly big number.

No one wants to burden their children with huge college debts, but consider that the time, money, and attention you divert from your retirement savings could leave you outliving your money in retirement. This could cause you to become an even bigger burden to your children later on.

That's why my advice is to prioritize your retirement savings first, and once that plan is in place, save what you can to help your children with college. Personally, I think there are some distinct advantages when youngsters save, work, and contribute toward their own educations. This is an opportunity to start teaching lessons to kids about saving for this future event. It's kind of like a precursor to retirement savings.

One piece of advice that sometimes gets me into a little hot water with parents, is urging them to slow down on helping their kids with college expenses. Too many people end up shooting themselves in the foot by spending hundreds of thousands of dollars paying for their kids' college so that their kids don't have to take on student loans. I appreciate that everyone wants to help their kids as much as possible, but you also need to be thinking about yourself and the lifestyle you want to live in retirement. Every dollar that is spent on college is another dollar that you were NOT able to save and compound for your retirement.

The problem is that college is just too expensive these days for a typical family to reasonably pay for all four years of college for all of their children. According to the College Board, the average cost of just tuition for the 2022–2023 school year was $39,400 at private colleges, $10,940 for state residents at public colleges, and $28,240 for out-of-state residents attending public universities. Add on top of that average room and board costs of $12,310 at four-year public schools and $14,030 at private schools.[9] This doesn't even include books and supplies and many other living expenses, such as a phone or car. Add these all together and the cost of college can easily exceed $100,000 per child.

I look at a family similar to my own with three children living in the state of Michigan and consider the full costs of sending those kids through a public in-state university. If each of the three children went to either the University of Michigan[10] or Michigan State University,[11] the yearly tuition cost is in the $16-20,000 range, depending on

---

[9] Collegedata.com. https://www.collegedata.com/resources/pay-your-way/whats-the-price-tag-for-a-college-education

[10] Financial Aid University of Michigan. "Cost of Attendance." https://finaid.umich.edu/getting-started/estimating-costs

[11] Michigan State University. "Cost and aid." https://admissions.msu.edu/cost-aid

university and class year. Add to that about $12-14,000 for room and board, the total yearly cost comes to around $28,000-34,000 per year. Of course, we hope our children are able to finish school within four years, but this plan doesn't always work out. It isn't hard to see how quickly these costs add up. Each child that graduates in four years is going to cost at least $100,000. Having three kids, that's $300,000. And this is a lower-end estimate because this assumes in-state tuition. If the children go to a private or out-of-state university, expect those costs to double. For most families, adding a $600,000 bill for college can kill their ability to save enough for retirement.

I have a hard time telling people that they need to have their children apply for student loans. But I know it is the right advice depending on the family's situation. I know people, myself included, would do anything for their kids. They don't want their kids to be saddled with student loans. Maybe their own parents paid their way through college, and they want to carry on the favor. But college is WAY more expensive than it was thirty or forty years ago.

It shouldn't be a given that the kids can attend college without contributing toward the costs. What if you spend all your money on college, and then there isn't enough for your retirement? I always hear from clients that the last thing they want is to become a burden on their kids. Well, if you don't have enough to live on because it was all spent on your kids' college educations, it is quite likely that this is exactly what will happen—you'll have to ask your kids for help. This is why I occasionally have to tell people the harsh reality, that they are overextending themselves financially by footing their kids' entire college bill. And I haven't even mentioned graduate school yet!

I find that there is an additional benefit that comes from not paying for all of your child's college: learning responsibility. My own parents didn't pay for all of my college expenses, even though they financially could have done so. In the case of myself and my brother, my parents let us both know early on that they'd pay tuition and board, but we were on our own for anything else. Ultimately, this left me responsible for about one-third of my college expenses. So, I had a choice, either get a job to earn the money to pay or start to take on student loans. I chose to work. Of course, college was a lot less expensive at that time than it is now, and that's another reason parents shouldn't feel obligated to match what their own family did, because an advanced education is so much more expensive today than it used to be.

In addition to working in college, I wasn't afraid to be resourceful either. If there was a party with a lot of cans laying around, I was the first one to volunteer to collect those cans. There was an understanding that whoever collected the cans and returned them to the store got to keep the money. Here in Michigan, we get ten-cents for every can returned. It was fairly easy to collect an extra $40 or $50 doing this.

Consider a client couple of mine who are both doctors. You can imagine how student debt can really pile up for a pair of doctors who have spent most of their lives attending school before ever making a dime. Obviously, the situation for a couple who are both doctors is an amplified example of the importance of handling debt correctly. She's great with money in general, but her husband is not. When I asked them about this, they said it's all about how they were brought up. His parents paid for all of his schooling, and while her parents could have paid for her college, they did not. They had her get loans; they had her go through that process of understanding how it all works, so that there's a financial commitment. Now she's the responsible one with money, and him, not so much. I tell people all the time, don't be scared of your child taking on a reasonable amount of student loans, because they can be a very valuable life lesson to your children.

Having your children take on some financial responsibility early on can be a very beneficial experience. And while I know that student loan debt is out of control in the US, and rates are way too high, but having your child have some skin in the game is important. I think her parents were smart in that they had her get some loans and made her take on that financial responsibility.

The most important lesson that came from me working in college to contribute to my costs, this was that I learned the value of a dollar. I learned the value of work. It gave me a strong work ethic. I think it is a very valuable lesson that I was given. The lesson was that my parents weren't going to hand me everything forever. Naturally, my parents would have done anything for me if I was in a bind, but they also wanted me to start gaining my own independence. If I wanted, I could have asked for help, but I didn't want to. It gave me a drive to start living on my own and being responsible for myself. I actually owe my parents a great deal for that realization. Paying one-third of my college costs has paid itself back in folds through the lessons I've learned. I think if you asked my mom, she'll probably tell you that I turned out OK.

The reality today is that students will have to take on student loans. I personally didn't take on student loans because I was able to make enough by working to pay my one-third. With the costs of college increasing at such a rapid rate, I don't think this is a realistic expectation anymore. About sixty years ago, my father started at Eastern Michigan University with the knowledge that he was totally responsible for all his college costs. He went to school and paid for his entire tuition and his living expenses while working concurrently. About twenty-five years ago, I was able to pay one-third by working. By now, the trend of increasing college costs has made it nearly impossible for a student to cover their own expenses with work. Kids won't be able to make enough income to pay much of the $100,000 college bill, so they will need to take on student loans to supplement what they earn.

I think the same type of lessons learned by working can also be learned with student loans. Loans and debt can certainly teach the value of a dollar. Having the responsibility to pay back loans is also valuable. I learned the lesson about debt when I first went to college and my parents had me get my own credit card. Then they simply said, "You can buy whatever you want with this credit card, but just remember, you are responsible for paying it all back every month." I learned the simple lesson of paying the bill each month before the due date. One time, I forgot to mail in my check to pay the bill. The next month, I got the statement in the mail and saw all the added late fees and interest. This had such an impact on me and was such a valuable lesson that I have never missed a credit card payment since. (Granted, the advent of automatic online payment now makes that task much easier!)

Debt, and the interest that accumulates on both credit cards and student loans, is another reminder of compounding. When someone neglects to pay a credit card for a few months, the high interest will make that credit card balance balloon to a huge number over a very short period of time. Each month with no payment, or with a minimum payment, will allow the debt to compound upon itself until it can be unsustainable to actually pay the debt back. Student loan statements can offer the same lessons on compounding. I've heard numerous times from folks that they were motivated to save and pay off debt early because they saw how they were paying more toward their loan interest than the principal itself! You can see this with a mortgage, as well. Even with lower interest rates, this can absolutely be the case because the debt is generally long-term, twenty to thirty years. Over that long period, compounding works its magic and forces the debtor to pay very little toward the principal in the early years. This is a simple fundamental lesson to watch your spending so that you can pay down the debt quicker. But at the heart of it, it just comes down to saving more, which brings us full circle to learning to save more for retirement.

CHAPTER 6

Social Security

The two most common questions that come up in relation to retirement are these: 1.) When can I afford to stop working?, and 2) When should I start collecting Social Security benefits?

For almost everyone except the wealthiest individuals, these two questions are inextricably intertwined. That's because, if you are still working and you haven't yet reached your full retirement age, which for most of us is sixty-six or sixty-seven years old, there's a significant disadvantage to starting to collect Social Security. If you're still working, you'll face a significant reduction in your Social Security benefits because of the earnings penalty. That penalty means that if you earn more than a very small amount—just $21,240 ($1,770 per month) in 2023[12]—Social Security deducts money from your benefit payment. For anyone collecting Social Security before their full retirement age, those benefits are reduced by $1 for every $2 earned above that limit. Once you hit your full retirement age, there's no limit on earnings while still being eligible to collect your full Social Security retirement benefit.

So, that's a warning sign. If you need to work and simultaneously collect Social Security before your full retirement age, you're probably in financial trouble. Otherwise, I've never seen a circumstance where it would be wise to take Social Security and work

---

[12] Social Security Administration. "Receiving Benefits While Working." https://www.ssa.gov/benefits/retirement/planner/whileworking.html#:~:text=If%20you%20are%20younger%20than,2022%2C%20that%20limit%20is%20%2419%2C560.

before your full retirement age. It just doesn't make sense unless you're terminally ill, at which point, you sadly might as well take the money because there's less of a chance you'll reach your full retirement age.

Social Security Basics

While you're working and saving, Social Security is pretty simple: you work, pay your FICA tax (which includes Social Security), and the Social Security Administration tracks your earnings.

Your benefit amount is based on an average of your highest-earning thirty-five years. You don't need to pick investments, make contributions, or do anything else.

Even for wealthy families, considering the optimal Social Security strategy is critical in order to maximize the benefit that you paid into throughout your working career. Nobody likes to leave money on the table.

Claiming Social Security

When it comes to claiming Social Security, things get more complicated. There are literally hundreds of ways to file for Social Security, but most of those options do not apply to folks born after 1954.[13] Some of those maximization strategies won't work for younger people. But even with all those options, most people haphazardly guess when they should take Social Security. It's usually based on when they happen to need the money, or it coincides exactly with their retirement date. For most people, they're simply choosing a date to start collecting, and that's about it. There's no real strategy or thought behind the decision.

The one thing to understand about Social Security is that the "best" way for you to take Social Security is really just a best guess. There are several unknown factors, the most important of which being, how long will you live? Nevertheless, if you're a single person, there aren't as many choices so the decision is simpler. In this case, you can consider your employment and savings situation, combined

---

[13] Social Security Administration. "Filing Rules for Retirement and Spouses Benefits."
https://www.ssa.gov/benefits/retirement/planner/claiming.html

with an estimate of your life expectancy based on health factors and family history, then choose a date to start collecting Social Security benefits.

Deferring to age seventy can be the best move, but if you don't live a long life, then it's not the best move. What if you take your benefit earlier, reinvest that money, and do really well with it? Then you actually can do better by taking Social Security earlier. You have to consider many factors between inflation, your life expectancy, your rate of return, and so on.

When making the decision on when to collect Social Security, there are three main points of consideration. One is how long do you expect to live? How long would you be collecting benefits? On that question, we just have to make a best guess. In fact, on all of these points, we really have to make educated assumptions because no one has that crystal ball into the future.

Another other question is, what is the time value of money? How much do you anticipate making on your money if you collect Social Security earlier? If you could make 6-percent on your investments compared with an 8-percent increase by delaying your benefits, you could end up with more money by taking the money early, because you're investing and growing that cash over a longer period of time.

To Defer or Not to Defer

Rather than collecting while they're working, a lot of people want to defer Social Security payments until they're seventy-years-old. That's the point at which you'll receive your highest monthly payment amount. For instance, if you were born in February 1960 and earned $100,000 in 2020, your normal benefit would be about $2,503 when you retire at Full Retirement Age, which is considered age sixty-seven for those born in 1960 or later. Retire five-years earlier at age sixty-two, and your benefit is cut to $1,752, which is 70-percent of the benefit provided at Full Retirement Age. But if you wait three-years to file a claim when you're seventy-years-old, your monthly payment would be $3,104.

People generally think it's smart to defer; they think they will get more money by delaying. Maybe they heard about the so-called "8-percent earnings" that they get by waiting. They don't realize that it's not real earnings. You're not getting paid 8-percent interest on your normal benefit amount; you're just getting a higher, delayed payout because you're letting the government hold onto your money longer.

Yes, you'll get a higher payout every month if you defer until age seventy, but you also didn't take money for the entire previous 36-months. In this example, you skipped receiving more than $90,000 in order to collect $600 more per month when you reach seventy-years-old. You'll need to collect that higher benefit for more than twelve-and-a-half years before you break even. At that point, you'll be over eighty-two years old. And that's not taking into account anything you could've earned by investing that money, or what you've lost if you end up taking cash out of your retirement investments while you're waiting for the higher benefit payment to kick in.

For example, if you start taking Social Security and leave your 401(k) or IRA alone, those retirement investments continue to grow, which can give you a better return than if you start taking 401(k) or IRA withdrawals in order to defer Social Security.

You don't have that issue if you keep working until age seventy, but remember, more than two-thirds of all U.S. workers retire before age sixty-five, and just 6-percent retire at age seventy or older.[14] So, whether you'll even be able to work until you're seventy is something you need to seriously consider, whether it's a matter of your health, being downsized, facing a layoff, or other career setback.

Let's say that you're sixty-seven years old, you're at full retirement age and you retire. You need $8,000 a month for your living expenses. Then say you've got a pension that's paying $5,000 a month. Where is your other $3,000 going to come from? That $3,000 could either come from Social Security or it can come from your assets.

I like to ask people: "Do you want to spend your money, or do you want to spend the government's money?" When I ask it that way, the answer always is, "Oh, I would rather take the government's money!" At that point, we've leveled the playing field and can have a realistic discussion. That doesn't necessarily mean you want to wait until you're seventy, but it doesn't necessarily mean you should take your benefit right away, either. There are many more factors to consider.

---

[14] Employee Benefit Research Institute and Greenwald Research. 2021. "2021 Retirement Confidence Survey." https://www.ebri.org/docs/default-source/rcs/2021-rcs/2021-rcs-summary-report.pdf

The knee-jerk reaction that you'll work until you're seventy-years-old, or wait to collect a bigger Social Security payout, is based on fear. People are afraid that life spans are longer, and they're afraid of running out of money in retirement. The reason they're afraid is because they don't know if they will be financially secure if they stop working. The reason they don't have a sense of financial security, is because they haven't met someone who can show them a reasonable projection of what their retirement income will look like.

I commonly meet with people who have saved up millions of dollars, but still think they will run out of money in retirement. They don't know how to calculate how long their money will last. Maybe they've used a retirement calculator online that projects how much money you need to retire, but those online tools are overly simplistic and woefully inaccurate.

One of the most important things I do for people, is equip them with the knowledge that they have enough, that they can stop worrying, that they can retire, and that they will be OK.

When I first meet with someone, they'll commonly say something like, "My goal is to retire in five-years at my full retirement age of sixty-seven." Then we'll put together a financial plan that looks really comfortable. That starts the wheels turning in their minds. When we meet the following year, they might ask, "What happens if I look at retiring in a couple years instead, at age sixty-four?" Then I get a call a year after that, and they say, "OK, I'm ready to retire. Can we do it now?"

It happens all the time. I see people move their retirement dates forward based on knowing that they won't run out of money. They don't realize that they've done a really good job of saving, as long as we don't mess this up. As long as we have a reasonable investment discipline where we're investing in a way that creates income without too much risk, they're going to have smooth sailing through retirement.

It's Not that Simple

A lot of the anxiety about Social Security comes down to the fact that it's not so simple. As mentioned previously, there are hundreds of different ways to file for Social Security. Until recently, there was an option called "file and suspend" that many couples would use to maximize benefits by having the higher earner file for benefits, then suspend them, which allowed the lower-earning spouse to collect their spousal benefit—which is a share of your spouse's Social Security benefit—while they both waited to collect a higher, maximized benefit later. That might sound confusing, but no matter because that option has been eliminated. Its closest sibling, taking a restricted benefit, is still available if you were born on or before January 1, 1954. That allows a husband or wife to claim the spousal benefit while allowing their own personal benefit to continue increasing.

One of my clients is a couple who were both about sixty-seven years old. The husband was collecting Social Security, and the wife was trying to defer her benefit until she turned seventy. But their income was tight only drawing his Social Security and pension. They figured they had no choice but to start withdrawing from investments. But there was actually a better plan. I explained that she could use the restricted benefit strategy by collecting a spousal benefit now, without affecting the deferral of her own Social Security. The spousal benefit ended up adding $1,100 to their monthly income, essentially for free. She was still able to defer her Social Security until age seventy, and they got the best of both worlds.

For most people born after 1954, the spousal benefit is designed to provide some retirement income to a low-earning spouse or a stay-at-home spouse who didn't have enough income to qualify for their own Social Security benefits. A business owner could, for example, take all the business income in his or her own name, then have a husband or wife collect a spousal benefit.

A lot of people talk about Social Security strategies because Social Security is a significant portion of people's retirement income. But due to relatively recent law changes, it's become more simplified. The strategies are more cut and dry now. That doesn't mean you should ignore a Social Security analysis; this is still an important factor in retirement planning to make sure nothing is being overlooked in your situation.

While there is a group of people who believe that everyone should try to defer collecting benefits as long as possible (i.e., until age seventy), there is another group of people at the opposite end of the spectrum. They think Social Security is going to go away, and everyone should collect their benefits as soon as possible. As for me,

I'm in the middle. I don't think Social Security is going to disappear. For people who are about fifty-five or older, I believe they won't see any major change in their benefits. This population is now pretty close to retirement. They're already under the assumption that Social Security will provide a certain amount of benefit. The government is unlikely to change any laws that would impact this group's benefit.

For people younger than that, it is prudent to prepare for the possibility that Social Security may be reduced in some fashion. Politicians have to figure out how to make Social Security sustainable for the long-term. One option the government has is to reduce benefits, which I think is unlikely. Another option would be to raise taxes, which is something politicians are reluctant to do to their voting base. The third option is something tricky, which typically is how Congress gets these types of things done.

Previously, Congress reduced Social Security by taxing it in the 1980s. Now, if you're a married couple earning income between $32,000 and $44,000, half of your Social Security benefits are taxed as regular income. If you're earning more than $44,000, then up to 85-percent of your Social Security benefits are taxable. For single individuals, half of the benefits between $25,000 and $34,000 are taxable, and 85-percent is taxable if you make more than $34,000.[15] This means that pretty much everyone I meet with is paying income tax on 85-percent of their Social Security benefits.

Back when this change was passed, somebody earning $44,000 a year was making a pretty decent income. Most people weren't subject to being taxed on all their Social Security. But now nearly everyone is. By increasing taxes, legislators can say they technically haven't cut benefits, but really, they have because you're essentially giving back some of that Social Security income in the form of taxes.

Another tactic is changing the way inflation is calculated to increase benefits, since Social Security payments increase over time based on inflation. Another obvious approach is to keep raising the full retirement age, just like when it increased from fifty-five years to sixty-five years to sixty-seven years old. I believe that's going to happen again.

This appears to be the most likely scenario for reducing the government's obligation to pay out Social Security benefits. First, it

---

[15] Social Security Administration. "Income Taxes and Your Social Security Benefit." https://www.ssa.gov/benefits/retirement/planner/taxes.html

can be implemented without necessarily reducing payments to those already collecting Social Security. Second, it can be gradually implemented based on the recipient's year of birth. Just as was done in previous iterations, the full retirement age could increase by two-months for every year younger you are. For example, if you were born in 1959, your full retirement age is sixty-six and ten-months. But if you were born in 1960, your full retirement age is two-months later, at age sixty-seven. Being born one-year later led to full Social Security benefits being paid out two-months later.

Many people feel this is the "fairest" way of implementing a change to Social Security because there is no distinctive cutoff date that dramatically changes everyone's Social Security. It will have a more gradual effect, which in theory, will allow younger people to adapt to the law change.

The Longevity Question

The big question that hovers over anyone's decisions about retirement saving and when to retire and claim Social Security benefits, is the question, "How long are you going to live?" That's the primary factor that influences the outcome of all these decisions. Of course, it also happens to be life's biggest unknown.

When it comes to how long your money needs to last, I always say: It's better to be overprepared and not need it, than underprepared and need it. Many financial advisors recommend planning for your money to last until your life expectancy, which is a best guess based on your health, how long family members lived, and so on. But what if you outlive that age?

A few years back, I got a call from someone seeking advice for his father. I asked how I could help. He said, "My dad just turned eighty-five. And he's doing really well health-wise." Doesn't sound like a problem, right? He continued, "My dad's advisor put together Dad's financial plan when he retired twenty-years ago. Dad's dad and uncle both lived until their mid-eighties, so he figured his life expectancy would also be around age eighty-five. The advisor designed Dad's plan based on his life expectancy of eighty-five. Now, Dad is eighty-five and is about to run out of money! What should we do?"

This was a conundrum. It's very difficult to turn a situation around when the money has already been spent. Unfortunately, at that point, the only options for this family were either the son helps his father financially, or his dad dramatically reduces his lifestyle.

This is why I stress the importance of planning for a longer life expectancy than your instinct suggests. You don't want to end up in a similar situation where you outlive your money. The truth is, we simply don't know how long we're going to live, and we don't want to be on the wrong side of that equation. If the dad's life expectancy was age eighty-five, I would have designed a plan so his money lasted until at least age ninety-five.

Consider Social Security again. All the payouts at various ages are based on life expectancy tables provided by the government. The benefits are pretty accurate according to how long the average American lives. The government is tracking this data and making sure that, on average, most people are collecting the same amount over the course of their retirements. But you don't know if that data represents your specific situation. You may be average, above average, or below average in terms of life expectancy.

What I've found most often is, the average working American decides to collect Social Security when they stop working. It's not always the most strategic or optimized approach, but it is sensible if that person needs to generate income.

Some of my clients still have pensions; some have partial pensions that were frozen in plans years ago. But Social Security is the only true pension that most people have, yet it's not enough to pay most people's bills. Years ago, it was commonplace to face a retirement where 40-percent of income came from Social Security, 40-percent came from a pension, and 20-percent came from their own savings. Well, now that pension is generally gone. Now the ratio is more like 35-percent from Social Security and 65-percent from your own sources. If you're only using stocks to generate that income, that can be a recipe for disaster.

This is the reason why stable income generation and having a truly diversified portfolio are so important. So much of your income will be dependent on the income generated by your portfolio of investments. As you'll learn in the next chapters, incorporating stocks, bonds, non-correlated assets, and fixed annuities to reduce volatility is critically important to any successful retirement.

CHAPTER 7

You'll Need More, Not Less

The common belief about retirement is that you should replace 80-percent of the living expenses you had while you were working. While it's true that some costs do go down in retirement—you're not commuting to work each day, eating lunch out, or maintaining a work wardrobe—the truth is that most people don't cut their expenses in retirement by much, if at all.

Think about it: When do you spend the most money during the week? Is it on Monday, when you're catching up on all the work that didn't get done last week, eating lunch at your desk, and then running home? No, it's on Saturday, when you have lots of time on your hands to start projects and entertain yourself. Now think about this: When you retire, every day is like a Saturday.

So, if you're only going to spend 80-percent of what you've been spending during your working years in retirement, where are you going to make cuts? How are you going to cut out the 20-percent?

When considering retirement, a lot of people say, "My expenses will be significantly reduced in retirement. I won't need two cars. I won't be driving downtown every day. I won't spend as much on gasoline. I won't be buying lunch. I won't need to buy suits or dresses or pantyhose." Gas and clothing are the two expenses that people regularly mention when this idea comes up, but how much of your budget is really consumed by gas and clothing?

Is that really 20-percent of your spending? It's probably not even close to that much. If you're going to follow that 80-percent approach, you're likely making an incorrect assumption. The idea that when you retire, you're going to spend 80-percent of your pre-retirement expenses, is highly inaccurate for most people.

People don't decrease their spending, especially not at the beginning of retirement. I call that point the honeymoon phase of retirement, because you'll probably see your spending actually *increase* for a period of time. When retirement is new, you are excited to have free time to do the things you didn't have time to do while you were working, like golfing every day or finally taking that vacation you've been dreaming of for years. Generally, this phase of heightened spending lasts between three-months to two-years of retirement. When that honeymoon phase subsides, people ultimately get into a groove with their daily routines and don't travel or eat out as much. So, their spending stabilizes back toward the norm and is closer to their pre-retirement spending.

Some people resist the thought that their expenses won't decrease much in retirement, and they present the argument: "But I will have my mortgage paid off, so my expenses will go down." This is one specific line item that must be considered individually. Paying down a mortgage is not really an expense; it is repayment of debt. Debt payments should be calculated differently than everyday expenses.

Healthcare

And, of course, there's healthcare, which can be one of the largest expenses in retirement. Fidelity estimated that in 2023, the average retired couple (age 65) will need $315,000 in current dollars for medical expenses during retirement, and that doesn't even include the costs of long-term care.[16]

Healthcare is one of those topics that's hard to talk about because it is constantly changing. Healthcare has increased so much in cost, and we don't know how long it will continue in the same way. There may be changes to the laws or structure of Medicare, Social Security, and other provisions. Some sort of change seems inevitable because

---

[16] Fidelity. June 21, 2023. "How to plan for rising health care costs." https://www.fidelity.com/viewpoints/personal-finance/plan-for-rising-health-care-costs#:~:text=How%20much%20is%20needed%20for,health%20care%20expenses%20in%20retirement.

there's not enough taxpayer money currently to fund everything that's needed as lifespans increase, medical technology expands, and the wave of Baby Boomers enters their later years in life.

It's a great unknown and, while I don't like to stoke unnecessary fear or use scare tactics, there's just not a good solution other than having more money. The big frustration is that there's no way now to really know what will happen, other than the harsh reality that healthcare is likely to be a big part of your overall retirement spending.

Everybody is so worried about healthcare, but they're really worried about the *future* of healthcare policy and costs, which is unknown. There's only so much you can do now beyond just saving. In the meantime, don't be scared to spend some money and enjoy your first years of retirement. This is the time to do fun things and enjoy your time. Don't let the fear of potential future healthcare costs change how you wish to live your life.

I try to take a lesson from my own circumstances. My dad had a long career as a teacher. He finally retired, then died six months later, so he never had much chance to enjoy his retirement. Of course, that's not typical because, on average, if you live to be about sixty-years-old, the actuarial statistics tell us that you're highly likely to live at least another twenty-five years. That's why I tell people to enjoy their retirement, to be responsible with their money, but enjoy it.

Right now, it's the year-to-year healthcare costs that change, making that something you're going to have to reconsider and adjust every few years. If healthcare increases much more in the coming years, it's increasing that much more for lots of people. At a certain point, change will have to come.

A good option to consider now is one of the Medicare supplement plans, which cover most of the expenses not covered by Medicare. This makes medical costs much more predictable and affordable than people think.

Take the case of a sixty-five year old non-smoking husband and wife living in Birmingham, Michigan. For plan G, which covers virtually all expenses outside of a yearly $240 deductible in 2024, the monthly premium would be approximately $130 for the husband and $120 for the wife, which comes to $250 per month or $3,000 per year. Granted, there are some additional costs of Medicare Part B itself and this cost varies based on income, but most people don't notice that cost because it generally comes out directly from their monthly Social Security income. Now, as you get older, the Medicare supplements will get more expensive, but not outrageously so. Looking at an eighty-year-old couple, the monthly premium would be $200 for the husband and $180 for the wife. An additional $230 per month isn't insignificant, but it is affordable for most people who have been disciplined in their savings. At age ninety, the premiums rise to about $250 for the husband and about $215 for the wife, for a total of $465 per month.[17]

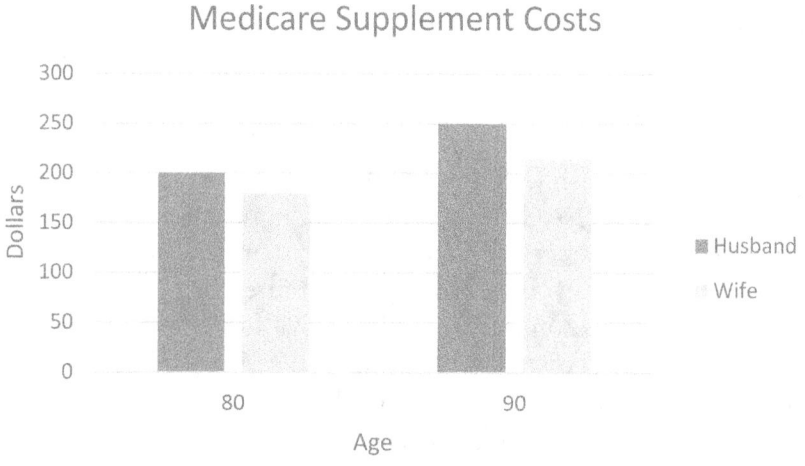

When it comes to your retirement lifestyle and timing, a lot of that comes down to your health. In some cases, your physical condition and any ailments narrow your choices while, for others, good genes, healthy habits, and luck leave you with more options. Either way, once you're into retirement, you don't want to risk having healthcare costs derail your years of disciplined financial efforts. Retirees with health issues should make sure they can get the benefits they need, and even the healthiest folks need to be protected from the financial havoc that can come with just one accident or diagnosis.

---

[17] Medicare.gov. "Supplement Insurance (Medigap) Plan G policies." https://www.medicare.gov/medigap-supplemental-insurance-plans/#/m/plan-policies/MEDIGAP_PLAN_TYPE_G?fips=20177&zip=66614&year=2022&lang=en

Even for those who have saved well for retirement, it is very common to want to continue working until age sixty-five so they can transition from employer health insurance straight to Medicare coverage. People realize that purchasing individual health insurance is very expensive and adds up month after month, year after year. Waiting until age sixty-five to retire for the sake of healthcare coverage, is much more common today than it was even five years ago.

In general, people are very concerned about long-term care. But the estimated percentage of people who will need long-term care is vastly exaggerated. The typical message people hear is that about 70-percent of people will need long-term care at some point in their lives.[18] The key is, "at some point in their lives." I played basketball in high school, and I had long-term care because I injured my ankle and had to go through physical therapy at a rehabilitation facility. In doing so, I became part of that 70-percent statistic, but I was only seventeen-years-old at the time. The statistics show that 37-percent of people utilizing long-term care services are under the age of sixty-five, which means those people probably aren't in a nursing home.[19]

Medicare

When it comes to Medicare, a lot of people think that the Medicare process is some huge, unwieldy process. It doesn't need to be as complicated as people think. There is a seven-month window when most Americans enroll in Medicare. This window starts three months before your birth month, and ends three months after your birth month. So if you were born in July, you can enroll as early as April 1st or as late as October 31st. You want to make sure to enroll within that seven-month period.

The two primary pieces of coverage are Medicare Part A, which is hospitalization, and Medicare Part B, which is regular health insurance. There also is Part D, which is the benefit that provides prescription drug coverage.

---

[18] LongTermCare.gov. February 18, 2020. "How Much Care Will You Need?" https://acl.gov/ltc/basic-needs/how-much-care-will-you-need
[19] LongTermCare.gov. August 2, 2021. "Understanding Long-Term Care." https://acl.gov/ltc/basic-needs

The most common misconception I find with my pre-retirement clients is that people assume they could have sky-high medical bills at age sixty-five or later, which frankly isn't true. Once you turn sixty-five, you have Medicare and, if you have assets, you get a Medicare supplement plan. As mentioned previously, the Plan G supplemental plan (also known as Medigap, Medicare Supplement, or MedSupp) covers every expense that Medicare doesn't cover under Parts A and B, with the exception of the $240 annual deductible as of 2024.[20]

There are a total of ten Medicare Supplement plans, ranging from Plans A through N, all with slightly different coverages and benefits. Premiums for each of these unique plans vary by location and age.[21] These payments often range from about $100 to $300 per month. That's not a crippling expense for most people when you consider that some hospitals will charge a hundred dollars for a bandage or an aspirin!

With most Medicare supplement plans, subscribers won't have any issues. Where you can potentially get into trouble is with a Medicare Advantage Plan, also known as Part C. With this plan, you could end up responsible for huge medical bills. People get enticed with Medicare Advantage because it advertises free or low-cost monthly premiums. It's the old adage that if it sounds too good to be true, it probably is. While the monthly premiums are low, the coverage could backfire when you ultimately need expensive care.

If you have built up money in savings and investments over the years, it is generally recommended to go with Plan G (Medicare Supplement) and avoid Part C (Medicare Advantage). Plan G has higher monthly premiums compared to Plan C, but it provides much more extensive coverage should you need it. As you age, you are more and more likely to need the kind of coverage that Plan G provides.

---

[20] CMS.gov. October 12, 2023. "2023 Medicare Parts A & B Premiums and Deductibles 2023 Medicare Part D Income-Related Monthly Adjustment Amounts." https://www.cms.gov/newsroom/fact-sheets/2023-medicare-parts-b-premiums-and-deductibles-2023-medicare-part-d-income-related-monthly

[21] Medicare.gov. "Supplement Insurance (Medigap) Plan G policies." https://www.medicare.gov/medigap-supplemental-insurance-plans/#/m/plan-policies/MEDIGAP_PLAN_TYPE_G?fips=20177&zip=66614&year=2022&lang=en

Plan G provides guarantees that nothing catastrophic will happen to you financially in retirement as it relates to healthcare.

Some people get into a bad situation because they start retirement on a low-cost Medicare Advantage plan, thinking they can switch into a Medicare Supplement plan down the road during open enrollment. However, your initial Medicare enrollment is the only time that you are guaranteed acceptance into Plan G. If you want to switch later, you will be subjected to medical underwriting by the insurance company. If your medical records are of any concern, you could be denied.

In 2023, most people don't pay Part A premiums, according to the federal CMS.gov website. People who didn't pay enough Medicare taxes while working or paid none, would pay $274 or $499 monthly, depending on how many quarters you worked. Those who worked and paid into Medicare under 30 quarters pay the higher amount, whereas those who worked 30 to 39 quarters pay the reduced amount.

The Part B premium for 2024 is $174.70 a month but can be higher depending on income. It maxes out at $594.00 a month for individuals earning $500,000 or more, or for joint filers earning $750,000 or more. People who are married but file separately hit the maximum monthly premium with a taxable income of $397,000 or more.[22] There are slightly different plans offered in Massachusetts, Minnesota, and Wisconsin.

---

[22] Ibid.

Medigap Benefits	Medigap Plans									
	A	B	C	D	F*	G	K	L	M	N
Part A coinsurance and hospital costs up to an additional 365 days after Medicare benefits are used up	Yes	Yes	Yes	Yes	Yes	Yes	Yes	Yes	Yes	Yes
Part B coinsurance or copayment	Yes	Yes	Yes	Yes	Yes	Yes	50%	75%	Yes	Yes***
Blood (first 3 pints)	Yes	Yes	Yes	Yes	Yes	Yes	50%	75%	Yes	Yes
Part A hospice care coinsurance or copayment	Yes	Yes	Yes	Yes	Yes	Yes	50%	75%	Yes	Yes
Skilled nursing facility care coinsurance	No	No	Yes	Yes	Yes	Yes	50%	75%	Yes	Yes
Part A deductible	No	Yes	Yes	Yes	Yes	Yes	50%	75%	50%	Yes
Part B deductible	No	No	Yes	No	Yes	No	No	No	No	No
Part B excess charge	No	No	No	No	Yes	Yes	No	No	No	No
Foreign travel exchange (up to plan limits)	No	No	80%	80%	80%	80%	No	No	80%	80%
Out-of-pocket limit**	N/A	N/A	N/A	N/A	N/A	N/A	$5,560 in 2019 ($5,880 in 2020)	$2,780 in 2019 ($2,940 in 2020)	N/A	N/A

All this being said, we haven't yet discussed the wild card of retirement health care expenses: prescription drug costs. Prescription drug costs are covered by Medicare Part D. However, similar to Medicare Part B, Medicare will only cover a portion of your prescription drug costs. The remainder will need to be covered out of pocket, or with a Part D plan. Part D plans are relatively inexpensive and keep the costs of most prescription drugs very reasonable.

It is very important to purchase a Part D plan when you first become eligible, even if you don't currently take any medications. For each month you are not signed up for Part D after age sixty-five (or after your qualifying employer coverage ends), you will be penalized 1%. This means that your Part D premiums will be *permanently* higher by 1% for every month you didn't have Part D. Delay getting Medicare Part D for just one year, and you will pay 12% more for Medicare Part D for the rest of your life!

In general, Medicare supplements are regulated by the government. The government sets standard rules and coverages that every plan must honor. For example, if you are shopping for a Medicare supplement plan (Plan G), the Plan G offered by one insurance company will have the exact same rules and coverages as another insurance company's Plan G. The only difference could be price. In this case, it is fine to choose a plan simply based on price because everything else will be equal.

However, Prescription Drug Plans (PDPs/Part D) does not work this way. Each insurance company may have a different structure in terms of coverage or co-pay. The specific medication being purchased can have a different cost between two different insurance companies. The good news is that you can shop for a new Part D plan every year. Your Medicare advisor can help you choose the best policy based on your specific medications and pharmacy preferences.

Regardless of which Plan D plan you choose, there are four coverage stages. The first is the Annual Deductible. Whether your plan has a deductible of $100 or $1,000, you must pay your expenses out of pocket until your deductible is met. Some plans may have a $0 deductible, in which case, your coverage starts right away. Once your deductible is satisfied, then you enter Initial coverage.

During the Initial coverage period, Medicare Part D pays for your prescriptions and you pay a co-pay or coinsurance. A co-pay is a fixed dollar amount, whereas coinsurance is a percentage of the drug's cost.

You will continue to pay this amount until you hit that year's Medicare initial coverage limit. For 2024, that limit is set at $5,030.

Once you spend up to that limit, then you enter the Coverage Gap (aka the "Donut Hole"). During this stage, Medicare pays 75-percent of the cost of your covered medications, and you pay the remaining 25-percent. You will continue on this arrangement until you hit $8,000 in out-of-pocket medication costs in a year, based on the 2024 figure. At that point, you enter the Catastrophic coverage phase.

Very few people fall into the Catastrophic category. Should this happen, Medicare fully covers your prescription drug costs after you've hit the $8,000 out-of-pocket amount toward medication. This will continue through the end of the year. The stages reset on January 1st.

Another factor impacting drug costs is the tiered system. Medicare classifies every medication as belonging to a tier numbered 1 through 5.

Tier 1 medications are the most inexpensive. They are the insurance company's "preferred generic drugs." Copays are minimal, usually in the $0 to $5 range. Tier 1 drugs are almost always excluded from the deductible, meaning that you go straight to a copay instead of paying out of pocket for Tier 1 medications.

Tier 2 drugs are still generic but are more expensive than Tier 1. Some plans exclude Tier 2 drugs from the deductible, but this is something to consider when shopping for a Part D plan. If your medication is subject to deductible, you will have to pay the full cost of that medication until your deductible is met. If it is excluded from the deductible, you just pay the minimal copay instead of having to meet the deductible first.

We start seeing brand-name medications in Tiers 3 and 4. Tier 3 consists of "preferred brand drugs" and Tier 4 consists of "non-preferred brand drugs." These tiers are increasingly more expensive than the previous ones, and you will pay the full cost of your prescription until your plan's deductible is met.

Specialty drugs are introduced in Tier 5. These types of medications are used to treat chronic or severe conditions, such as cancer, H.I.V., autoimmune diseases, and more. Usually, you need a prior authorization to receive these drugs, and you will likely receive only a limited supply at a time. These drugs are very expensive and can be financially burdensome, even devastating, for some. This is where financial assistance through pharmaceutical assistance programs (PAPs) can be a tremendous benefit. The pharmaceutical companies that manufacture specialty drugs often have PAPs available that your doctor's office can help facilitate. These financial-assistance programs are typically available to everyone regardless of income or financial status.

A stickier healthcare issue comes up when potential retirees are too young for Medicare. Frequently, when families come to me and get a full picture of their finances, we determine that they can retire sooner than they expected. If they're not eligible for Medicare yet and have been self-employed or running their own business, it's not too much of an issue, because they're already paying for their own healthcare and know exactly what the cost is. If they're leaving a job where they've held employer-paid healthcare, however, healthcare premiums leave them with a sense of sticker shock. In fact, that can push people to reconsider retirement altogether until they turn sixty-five and can utilize Medicare coverage.

But when we actually crunch the numbers and run an analysis, I can help them determine whether they should retire at sixty-two or sixty-five based on healthcare costs. If a married couple needs to spend $20,000 a year for healthcare coverage and they're retiring at sixty-two, then they need to cover their healthcare premiums for three years. In that case, we can incorporate that extra $60,000 healthcare expense into their financial plan. Then we can get them back to a situation where they realize, "We can actually retire earlier than we had thought!"

Long-Term Care

When it comes to long-term care, people are either really concerned about the potential cost or not concerned at all. Some people think "It won't happen to me; I won't need long-term care," or "I'll just spend my own money if I have to deal with it." Some people simply insist, "No one is taking me to a nursing home," even though they may not have family members able to care for them, or that they may need skilled nursing care, physical rehabilitation, or other specialized treatments. The worst possible response comes from people who assume, "The government will take care of me," without understanding that they'll need to spend down almost all of their assets—including those of their spouse—and hope they can find a bed in a Medicaid facility, and that the quality of care and the quality of the facility will be acceptable. Even when they can keep their home, the property could be subject to being claimed by Medicaid after their death. All these forms of denial can be dangerous, not only to a retiree's finances, but also to a spouse, children, or to their own quality of healthcare. I find that once people have seen a loved one need long-term care, they suddenly become very concerned about how to handle it personally.

There are two big reasons people should want to address long-term care. One is, they don't want to be a burden on their family. If something happens, they don't want their kids having to rearrange their lives to take care of them. Simply not being a burden to loved ones is a huge motivator.

Another major reason to address long-term care is to avoid a spouse becoming the caretaker. Not only is this emotionally difficult, but it often results in the spouse hiring in-home help, which can drain the family's finances. The surviving spouse can end up in a bad financial situation as a result.

For people who are single and have no children, a common assumption is that they'll simply spend down their assets, then go into a Medicaid-assisted care facility. In this case, long-term care coverage helps afford a nicer facility with a better overall living experience.

Many people are conflicted about buying long-term care insurance for a variety of reasons. One reason is the unknown of whether you will need long-term care during your lifetime. In order to have an affordable premium amount, you need to purchase a long-term care policy long in advance of ever needing the coverage, typically sometime between the ages of fifty and sixty-years-old. If you don't need the policy until you're eighty-years-old, for example, you've been paying a lot of money toward premiums for twenty-years or more.

Another issue is that long-term care premiums can be adjusted higher, so they can get more expensive as you age. Often times, premiums continue to rise over time such that it becomes prohibitively expensive at older ages, which is precisely when it is most likely that you would need the coverage. In this case, there is a decision to make: either continue making increasingly higher premium payments, reduce the amount of care that the policy covers, or drop the policy completely, leaving the individual without any protection at all.

Many times, a big concern people have with long-term care is, "I'm putting all this money into the policy, and I could never end up using it, and it's a black hole for my money." Unless you or your spouse become sick enough to need an extended amount of long-term care, it can seem like those years of premium payments were wasted.

Some companies work around that by offering survivorship life insurance that primarily functions as long-term care coverage. Survivorship insurance—which also is called "second-to-die insurance"—simply means that the policy pays out only after the last surviving spouse passes away. In its basic form, couples use the coverage to create an inheritance or to pay off debts or taxes or other expenses in their estate. A few insurers allow that insurance to function as a long-term care policy for both spouses. Even if one of them passes away, the long-term care continues for the surviving spouse. If neither spouse uses the long-term care benefits, then the policy pays out a death benefit to the beneficiaries when the last surviving spouse passes away. If only a portion of the death benefit amount has been paid out for long-term care services, then the remaining balance is paid as a death benefit to the beneficiaries.

For example, let's say you buy a $250,000 joint survivorship policy that will pay out unlimited amounts of long-term care coverage. If you and your spouse end up needing $250,000 in long-term care, then you have exhausted the death benefit—there's nothing left to pay out after you both die. If you don't need long-term care, the death benefit remains intact and is paid after the last spouse passes away. So, you're covered for long-term care as a couple, but if you and your spouse never end up needing long-term care, then your beneficiaries can collect the death benefit.

The premium on this kind of policy can be structured so that it's paid over ten years, fifteen years, or you continually pay a premium as long as you live. Typically, I structure the payments over ten years, after which you're fully covered and don't have to put in another dime. The premium amount depends on age and other factors, but generally you pay about $250,000 to get $250,000 in death benefits, structured as $25,000 per year over a 10-year period. But, unlike so many long-term care policies, the other thing this combined survivorship coverage offers is that as soon as you set up the account, you're locked in at a certain price and coverage level, and that never changes.

Another way to look at this is using a more traditional life insurance policy that is based on one person's life, rather than two. With individual life insurance with long-term care benefits, you have a death benefit for a certain amount. That bucket of money is accessible for long-term care as well. A lot of times, this is a $500,000 policy, and typically you can take out up to 2-percent per month. Two percent of $500,000 is $10,000 a month, which could be accessed for long-term care expenses. Being able to take out 2-percent per month covers you for fifty-months or four-years and two-months of coverage for nursing home care or whatever else is needed.

While your financial condition will always be a huge factor in making your retirement decisions, the lifestyle you want in retirement and your overall health outlook is going to be just as important in putting together a retirement plan that really works for you.

Let Yourself Spend...

One adjustment that a surprising number of people need to make in retirement, is they need to allow themselves to spend money. After a lifetime of saving, it's hard to break the habit of always squirreling away cash for the future by scrimping on your spending.

I recently had a client who's not retired yet, but has saved up a good amount of money to pay for college for his kids, and he talked about how hard it was to sell those investments. Over the years, he had researched and selected individual stocks and mutual funds after opening a brokerage account when each child was born and investing for them right away. It was hard to sell off the accounts because he was emotionally attached to those investments. But, of course, that's why he'd saved the money—so he could cash in the investments and send his kids off to college.

He told me, "I know it's going to be really hard once I retire to change my thinking of just focusing on accumulation to distribution and preservation."

This is something I talk about a lot. What we help people to do is move from the accumulation phase of their life, to the distribution and preservation phases. Making that transition is the most important time of your financial life. The first five-years of retirement is the most crucial to your finances, because this timeframe determines whether your retirement plan will succeed or not in the long-term. How you execute the transition, how the market is doing, and how your accounts do during these first five-years are very telling. This is where having a good, solid plan will give you the kind of financial independence everyone covets.

Another block to spending in retirement with some clients is they feel an obligation to leave a sizeable chunk of money behind to their children or grandchildren. What I typically tell these clients is that while it's natural to want to leave money behind for your kids, you want to make sure you're comfortable first. As we've discussed, the last thing anyone wants is to become a burden to their children. It's different with people who inherited money themselves. They want to pass money on to their kids because they had someone pass that money on to them. They don't want to be the one that ends the chain of family wealth.

...But Don't Overspend Prematurely

When the problem is over-spending, that issue doesn't suddenly crop up during the honeymoon phase or any other phase of retirement. Instead, it's that those individuals are spending too much in their pre-retirement lifestyle. And that lifestyle is unlikely to change in retirement.

As part of our retirement planning process, it is important to be honest about spending habits. It quickly becomes obvious when someone is spending more than they originally estimated with me. If a couple tells me they are spending what they have coming in from their paychecks each month and their savings accounts are not increasing, then I know that they are spending 100-percent of their net pay. If they tell me they are spending $6,000 per month, but their net take-home pay is $8,000, then we know there is a disconnect. If someone is spending $2,000 more per month than they thought, that discrepancy can have a very dramatic impact on retirement projections.

It is better to understand how much you are actually spending prior to retirement because it gives us the chance to adjust. It is generally difficult to make major lifestyle changes to lower expenses, but perhaps we can find a few minor changes in spending to implement, or maybe working another year or two will help get to a more comfortable retirement projection.

Don't Assume Lower Taxes

One big assumption people make about retirement, is they expect not only to spend less, but they expect to shift down to a lower tax bracket. But what if your working income is near the top of the 24-percent tax bracket, for example? That's more than $300,000 in income for a married couple. You might need a lot more than a 20-percent reduction in income to lower your tax bracket. Even then, you're only shifting from a 24-percent to a 22-percent tax rate under the current tax brackets.

2023 Tax Brackets
Taxes Due April 2024 or October 2024 with an Extension

Tax Rate	Single	Head of Household	Married Filing Jointly or Qualifying Widow	Married Filing Separately
10%	$0-$11,000	$0-$15,700	$0-$22,000	$0-$11,000
12%	$11,001-$44,725	$15,701-$59,850	$22,001-$89,450	$11,001-$44,725
22%	$44,726-$95,375	$59,851-$95,350	$89,451-$190,750	$44,726-$95,375
24%	$95,376-$182,100	$95,351-$182,100	$190,751-$364,200	$95,376-$182,100
32%	$182,101-$231,250	$182,101-$231,250	$364,201-$462,500	$182,101-$231,250
35%	$231,251-$578,125	$231,251-$578,100	$462,501-$693,750	$231,251-$346,875
37%	$578,126 or more	$578,101 or more	$693,751 or more	$346,876 or more

Source: IRS

Comparison of Current Income Tax Brackets (2023) to Former Income Tax Brackets (2017)

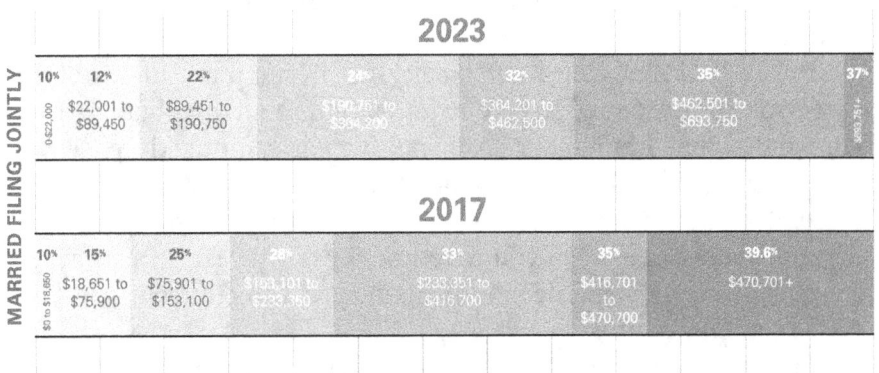

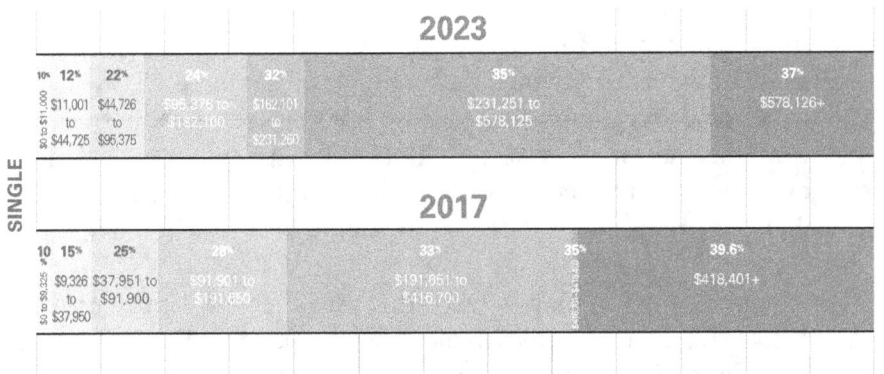

Sources:
IRS. Oct. 18, 2022. "IRS provides tax inflation adjustments for tax year 2023."
https://www.irs.gov/newsroom/irs-provides-tax-inflation-adjustments-for-tax-year-2023. Accessed Nov. 18, 2022.

Tax Foundation. Nov. 10, 2016. "2017 Tax Brackets."
https://taxfoundation.org/2017-tax-brackets/. Accessed Nov. 18, 2022.

If your taxable income is $250,000 now, you're paying $48,579 in federal tax. If your income drops down to $165,000, you're just barely into the 22-percent bracket, which lowers your tax bill to $28,179. So, you've saved about $20,000 in taxes but you had to reduce your income by one-third, $85,000. That difference between your income reduction and the tax savings—a whopping $65,000—is going to require a lot more than spending less on gasoline and work clothes.

Beyond all that, you'll eventually get to the point in retirement when you'll be required to take required minimum distributions from your Individual Retirement Accounts, which can quickly push you right back up into a higher tax bracket. Those distributions will be taxed at whatever the current tax rate is at that time, which you can't depend on knowing when you're retired for thirty years. Tax brackets get changed with some degree of frequency; sometimes it's in your favor, sometimes not.

I'm firmly convinced that tax rates have no choice but to increase moving forward. We are at historically low tax rates right now, and the national debt skyrocketed even further during COVID. The government will be forced to generate more tax revenue. That's why I tell people to start a Roth IRA if they qualify. They don't get the tax deduction now like they would with a regular IRA, but the growth and the withdrawals are all tax-free forever. This protects people from the risk of higher tax brackets in the future. Most people have far more money in tax-deferred accounts than they do in Roth accounts. This imbalance is precisely what creates the ticking tax timebomb that can derail your retirement.

Of course, we don't know when this tax hike will happen or what it will look like. But it is inevitable. The government has already set the precedent of high taxes many times in the past. Consider the 1980s. A married couple today earning $200,000 per year is in the 24-percent tax bracket. But if we inflation-adjust that income back to 1980 values, what tax bracket would you be in? Many people guess somewhere around 35-percent. But the answer is actually 54-percent! It's a pretty dramatic change—that tax bracket is more than double what it is today! If you were in the top tax bracket—a single filer earning over $390,000 or a married couple earning over $775,000 in today's dollars—you were in the 70-percent tax bracket!

1980 Tax Brackets[23] & 1980 Tax Brackets Inflation-Adjusted for Year 2022[24]

Tax Rate	Single Filers: 1980 Dollars	Married Filing Jointly: 1980 Dollars	Single Filers: Inflation-Adjusted to 2022 Dollars	Married Filing Jointly: Inflation-Adjusted to 2022 Dollars
0%	$0-$2,300	$0-$3,400	$0-$8,280	$0-$12,240
14%	$2,300-$3,400	$3,400-$5,500	$8,280-$12,240	$12,240-$19,800
16%	$3,400-$4,400	$5,500-$7,600	$12,240-$15,840	$19,800-$27,360
18%	$4,400-$6,500	$7,600-$11,900	$15,840-$23,400	$27,360-$42,840
19%	$6,500-$8,500		$23,400-$30,600	
21%	$8,500-$10,800	$11,900-$16,000	$30,600-$38,880	$42,840-$57,600
24%	$10,800-$12,900	$16,000-$20,200	$38,880-$46,440	$57,600-$72,720
26%	$12,900-$15,000		$46,440-$54,000	

---

[23] Tax-Brackets.org. "Federal Income Tax Brackets (Tax Year 1980.)" https://www.tax-brackets.org/federaltaxtable/1980

[24] Ian Webster. CPI Inflation Calculator. "$1 in 1980 is worth $3.60 today." https://www.in2013dollars.com/us/inflation/1980?amount=1#:~:text=Value%20of%20%241%20from%201980,cumulative%20price%20increase%20of%20260.20%25.

One dollar in 1980 would be equivalent to $3.60 in 2022 dollars. The average inflation rate over these 42 years is 3.1-percent, resulting in a cumulative increase of 260.2-percent.

Rate				
28%		$20,200-$24,600		$72,720-$88,560
30%	$15,000-$18,200		$54,000-$65,520	
32%		$24,600-$29,900		$88,560-$107,640
34%	$18,200-$23,500		$65,520-$84,600	
36%		$23,500-$28,800		
37%		$29,900-$35,200		$107,640-$126,720
39%	$23,500-$28,800		$84,600-$103,680	
43%		$35,200-$45,800		$126,720-$164,880
44%	$28,800-$34,100		$103,680-$122,760	
49%	$34,100-$41,500	$45,800-$60,000	$122,760-$149,400	$164,880-$216,000
54%		$60,000-$85,600		$216,000-$308,160
55%	$41,500-$55,300		$149,400-$199,080	
59%		$85,600-$109,400		$308,160-$393,840
63%	$55,300-$81,800		$199,080-$294,480	
64%		$109,400-$162,400		$393,840-$584,640
68%	$81,800-$108,300	$162,400-$215,400	$294,480-$389,880	$584,640-$775,440
70%	$108,300 or more	$215,400 or more	$389,880 or more	$775,440 or more

I'm not saying that taxes will necessarily go up that much in the future. But we must understand that taxes are really low today. And there's a big problem that people can have, even if they've been good savers and have a decent amount saved up in tax-deferred accounts.

Between Social Security, pension income, perhaps some investment income, inherited RMDs, and your own required minimum distributions, it is very easy for your income to creep up on you.

We see this very consistently with retirees. Consider an individual who contributed the maximum amount into their 401(k) every year of their working career. That is decades of contributions with compounded growth over that same timeframe. The RMDs will be substantial. When you're forty or fifty-five, you're not thinking about how that money is going to grow and get taxed in the future. You're just thinking about how you're being a good, responsible saver, and maybe the immediate tax deduction seems enticing at the time. Then you hit your early- to mid-seventies in age, and the government mandates that you start taking out a percentage of those accounts, and you'll have to pay regular income tax on that money. It can be shocking how much income and tax this creates to someone who never considered the tax impact. In order to avoid this scenario, it actually makes sense to pay taxes now, as opposed to waiting for the future when taxes could be much higher.

It should be noted that at the time of the publication of this book, current tax rates are set to expire. Provisions in the law stipulate that the Tax Cuts and Jobs Act (TCJA) sunsets on December 31, 2025, and if nothing changes, taxes will return to their previous higher rates. I do not expect any changes to this plan, because the government desperately needs more tax revenue, and the politicians leading the country at that time won't have to take the blame for raising taxes; it was already built into legislation that went into effect in 2018.

The most important thing to remember is that going from the accumulation phase of your life when you're working and saving and investing, to the distribution phase in retirement, is the absolute most important time in your financial life. That's why people need to have a plan, and if you've done a good job of saving over the years, that plan absolutely must incorporate tax strategy. A plan with thoughtful and tactical tax strategy provides the confidence to retire and spend more money than you thought you could, and/or it can allow you to retire earlier than you ever thought possible. Helping people do that gives me a tremendous sense of pride.

CHAPTER 8

Women and Retirement

Women should never settle for any kind of second-class financial future. However, in many cases, that's exactly what happens. Don't get me wrong, I know many women who are very financially savvy. But there are still ripples in society from the "old-school" mentality that men handled the household finances. This ideology can subconsciously pass down generations. Some women may feel intimidated by financial matters. Or, if a traditional belief is upheld, they may stipulate that their spouse should take care of financial decisions.

To me, that's just baffling. In my life, I have never been misled into thinking that women are incapable or inferior at handling finances. Both of my grandfathers died fairly young. My grandmothers handled everything on their own—and did a great job.

Marian, my maternal grandmother, lived in Virginia and was a widow for forty-years. She lived until she was ninety-four years old. She had no choice but to handle everything on her own for those four decades. I grew up seeing this, and never gave it a second thought. For that reason, I've never considered it out of the ordinary for women to manage money and, frankly, every other aspect of their lives.

Marian did more than just handle her own money. She also managed everything that happened within her estate, claimed whatever insurance was involved, and handled a lot of financial matters that go well beyond the plain vanilla chores of making sure the mortgage and the bills get paid on time.

One thing I can look back on and say about my grandmother, she not only took care of her household finances very well, but she was also smart enough to seek out an advisor who helped manage her investments and more advanced financial matters. That's the right way to do it, and it's what I encourage my clients to do. I can help with the financial part of your life, but you need to be in charge of your household budget.

On top of that, my wife, Erika, has always been financially savvy. She worked on the New York Mercantile Exchange, which is the leading marketplace for derivatives and other highly sophisticated financial instruments, such as oil futures, metals futures, energy futures, and agricultural commodities. She is a math wizard with extensive knowledge of business financials and tax strategies. No wonder I enthusiastically brought her into my business when we were engaged to be married!

It's always been my experience that women are more than capable of handling money and finances. Unfortunately, that's not how some people approach it. Consequently, women can get left behind. Even some financial advisors, both male and female, will talk predominantly to the male client, even when his wife is sitting right next to him! In a couple, both individuals need to feel involved, heard, and respected. Sure, one spouse may understand concepts better than the other, but it is very important that both spouses feel confident and comfortable with their financial plan.

It has been my experience in the financial world, generally speaking, that women tend to be more risk-averse than men—but women also are better investors, better at saving money, and better at paying down debt. They are also more inclined to ask for help and seek out a financial professional to manage their money. And, once again, that's why I find it puzzling that so many people think only men should handle the money, especially in a marriage. The truth is, if you really want the best long-term financial results, you would do the exact opposite and put women in charge!

I'm passionate about helping everyone—men, women, families, etc.—through their financial journeys towards retirement. However, women have specific concerns that are critical to address. In addition to the fact that women are more likely to live longer than men, they are also more likely to face poverty. Women age sixty-five and older are 80-percent more likely than men to be impoverished.[25] So, let's talk about what women are facing when it comes to finances.

Having the Tough Financial Conversations

There's usually one person in a couple who takes charge of the finances, and many times in our society, that just happens to be the man. This definitely doesn't have to be the case. Regardless of who is the financial alpha, it's important that both individuals are involved in the conversation and on the same page. You can't expect to be prepared for retirement if you both aren't part of the financial conversation.

Take a moment to consider what happens when the unthinkable occurs and a spouse passes away. Generally, it's the husband who passes away first, and the wife comes into the advisor's office with a stack of envelopes, not sure what to do next. Maybe she has a few details about their financial landscape, but she admits that her husband was the one taking care of these things. She wonders, will she be okay? Many times, the answer is yes, but it can be a scary situation to face during an overwhelming time.

Even if they haven't been in charge or highly involved with their financial matters as a couple, women often end up in charge, whether they like it or not. Sometimes this happens due to divorce, but more often it's because women are more likely to outlive their husbands.[26]

While living longer is usually, of course, a good thing, it also means more money is needed. For example, with aging comes increased costs of healthcare and prescription drugs. Maybe the widow will need to hire someone to provide in-home assistance and companionship. While the averages show that women live just two-

---

[25] statistica.com. 2022. "Poverty rate in the United States in 2020, by age and gender" https://www.statista.com/statistics/233154/us-poverty-rate-by-gender/

[26] Administration for Community Living. May 27, 2021. "Profile of Older Americans." https://acl.gov/aging-and-disability-in-america/data-and-research/profile-older-americans

years more than men, consider that the eight oldest people in the world are all women.[27] One statistic I find compelling, is that 80-percent of women die single, whereas 80-percent of men die married. This is a reflection that women live longer, and also that women tend to be a little younger than men when they get married.[28] I was also shocked to learn that the average age a wife becomes widowed is 59.4.[29]

It's one of life's most horrible days when a spouse passes away. But once the grief begins to lift, you'll realize that it's also the worst tax day of your life, too. That's because now you're filing as a single person, as opposed to married. That means your taxes can go up significantly, but for most people, the household spending does not decline much. There are a lot of fixed expenses—such as a mortgage or car payments—that don't change when a spouse passes away.

What does happen, is that the surviving spouse—usually a woman—loses one Social Security payment, which is the lower of the two payments the couple has been receiving. That can result in a significant loss of income. If the deceased spouse was collecting a pension, the widow will typically see that payment reduced by 35-percent or 50-percent if there was a survivor benefit, or if not, they will lose that pension income entirely.

That leaves a widow with less income and higher taxes, and now the money needs to last longer. At this point, they need to sit down with an advisor to figure out if they will be comfortable and what strategic actions will improve the situation. Of the three income sources people may have in retirement—Social Security, pensions, and savings—two are reduced after the death of a spouse. Meanwhile, savings need to last longer, expenses aren't necessarily cut

---

[27] Martin Armstrong. World Economic Forum. April 29, 2022. "How old are the world's oldest people?"
https://www.weforum.org/agenda/2022/04/the-oldest-people-in-the-world/
[28] Stacy Francis. Kiplinger. June 2, 2021. "Widows Move Forward on Their Own – But Not Alone." https://www.kiplinger.com/personal-finance/602892/widows-move-forward-on-their-own-but-not-alone.
[29] Kathleen M. Rehl. CNBC. March 6, 2020. "Recent widows need financial guidance after a spouse's death."
https://www.cnbc.com/2020/03/06/recent-widows-need-financial-guidance-after-a-spouses-death.html

significantly, and taxes will take a bigger bite out of the money you withdraw from taxable retirement and investment accounts.

However, this doesn't have to be the case. With advance planning, your financial landscape can look different.

Inviting Both Spouses to the Table

Talking with your spouse about finances is paramount (and the sooner, the better). But even more important is the psychological aspect of the situation. With almost every couple, there's going to be one person who is more involved with the finances. It's common for couples to shove aside discussions about their financial details. One big advantage of having an advisor is everything's in one place and, more importantly, you've got a professional looking at your whole financial picture, including Social Security, life insurance, healthcare, and investments. For the surviving spouse, it can be a tremendous relief to have someone like that in their corner, helping to make the many complicated financial decisions.

Even if one spouse is not fully involved in all the individual financial choices and decisions, it's still important to at least be present. In my practice, we ask that both spouses attend visits so they both know what's going on with their investments. It is very important that I have a relationship with both spouses, and that I can make sure both spouses understand what is happening with their money.

One of the issues that happens when one spouse—often a woman—hasn't been involved in a couple's financial planning, is that once they're left to sort matters out alone, they won't feel comfortable working with the financial advisor who's been handling their money for many years. In fact, 80-percent of widows fire their advisor in the first year after their spouse's death.[30] That just shouldn't happen. It's a sure sign that a foundation was never established between the advisor and other half of that couple.

---

[30] Stacy Francis. CNBC. November 22, 2021. "Op-ed: Recent widows need financial guidance after a spouse's death."
https://www.cnbc.com/2021/11/22/op-ed-recent-widows-need-financial-guidance-after-a-spouses-death.html

This kind of sudden change between advisors can be dangerous. The surviving widow is making a major change at a time when stability is the most important thing. Transferring assets to a new advisor at the wrong time could result in investment losses and tax liability. Even if that change happens during a bull market, the lag between moving an account from one advisor to another could mean the widow is missing out on share price gains while shopping around for a new financial manager.

What's more, if it's a sudden move to a new advisor, the surviving spouse might decide after a few years that she didn't make the right call, and then end up moving to yet another advisor. At every one of those transitions, there's an opportunity to incur expenses, taxes, and potential investment losses if not implemented properly. Things can fall through the cracks and disrupt the financial plan instead of making sure the money is being put to the best use in a long-term plan that incorporates retirement considerations.

Making Financial Decisions Together

With certain financial products, there will be spouse-specific options. It's crucial to be on the same page on these items so that your financial future is clear. Pensions, Social Security, life insurance, and annuity policies, all have the potential to impact the other spouse.

When it comes to pensions, it can be tempting to take the worker's life-only option. It's the bigger paycheck, but it doesn't leave anything to your spouse if you pass away first. Talk it over, because you don't want one of you to be left with nothing, especially if that person lives a long time. Though pensions aren't as common anymore, this is just one example of the items you'll want to talk about with your spouse.

One thing to consider is that it's not always possible for the woman to retire at the same time time as her husband, especially if she's a few years younger than him. She might need to continue working a few more years to make the financial situation work. Sometimes, it can be a situation where the husband has lost his job or has developed some kind of disability and can't work anymore. That's a fairly straightforward situation for a husband to retire sooner than the couple might have planned.

But it can get a little dicey when somebody says, "I'm going to retire now because I'm sixty-two and then you can keep working until you're sixty-two," when the wife is five-years younger than the husband. First off, there can be a little bit of what I call, "lifestyle resentment" there, because one spouse is retired while the other is still expected to bring home a paycheck.

But it also can get complicated financially. People can get tripped up because one spouse is collecting Social Security, which can throw off their tax situation on a joint tax return. The couple may assume the husband will get a certain Social Security benefit, but if the wife has her own income, his Social Security suddenly becomes taxable. The result is that they're not getting as much money as they expected. And it's not a small amount—once they cross the income threshold of $32,000 as a couple, they can face a tax hit on anywhere from half of his Social Security income to as much as 85-percent.

P.S. Remember, if you were a homemaker for quite a while, you may want to base your Social Security on your spouse's or ex-spouse's work history. Make sure you're getting your maximum benefit for your hard work, whether that work was put in inside or outside the home!

Things to keep in mind about Social Security Spousal Benefits:[31]

- Your benefit will be calculated as a percentage (up to 50-percent) of your spouse's earned monthly benefit at his or her full retirement age (FRA).
- For you to begin receiving a spousal benefit, your spouse must have already filed for his or her own benefits and you must be at least sixty-two years old.
- You can qualify for half of your spouse's benefits if you wait to file until your own FRA.
- Beginning your benefits earlier than your FRA will reduce your monthly check, but waiting to file until after FRA will not increase your benefits.

---

[31] Social Security Administration. "Retirement Planner: Benefits For You As A Spouse." https://www.ssa.gov/planners/retire/applying6.html.

For divorcees:[32]

- You may qualify to withdraw an ex-spousal benefit if:

    a) You were married to each other for a decade or more,
    b) AND you are at least sixty-two,
    c) AND you have been divorced for at least two years,
    d) AND you are currently unmarried,
    e) AND your ex-spouse is at least sixty-two years old (i.e., qualifies to begin taking Social Security).

- Your ex-spouse does not have to have filed for you to file on his or her benefit.
- Similar to spousal benefits, you can qualify for up to half of your ex-spouse's benefits if you wait to file until your FRA.
- If your ex-spouse dies, you may file to receive a widow/widower benefit on his or her Social Security record as long as you are at least age sixty and fulfill all the other requirements.

    f) This will not affect the benefits of your ex-spouse's current spouse

For widow's or widower's benefits:[33]

- You may qualify to receive as much as your deceased spouse would have received if:

    a) You were married to each other for at least nine months prior to his or her death,
    g) OR you would qualify for a divorced spousal benefit,
    h) AND you are at least sixty-years-old,
    i) AND you did not/have not remarried before age sixty.

- You may earn delayed credits IF your spouse hadn't already

---

[32] Social Security Administration. "Retirement Planner: If You Are Divorced." https://www.ssa.gov/planners/retire/divspouse.html.
[33] Social Security Administration. "Survivors Planner: If You Are The Worker's Widow Or Widower." https://www.ssa.gov/planners/survivors/ifyou2.html.

filed for benefits when he or she died.
- Other rules may apply if you are disabled or care for a deceased spouse's dependent or disabled child.

Keeping Track of Finances

Something that differs today from the financial situation my grandmother assumed, is the added complexity of finances. Multiple online accounts exist, all with their own logins. Often, there is no paper record or documentation.

My grandmother could have looked through the family checkbook and reviewed the records and gained a complete view of her entire financial picture. Today, there's automatic bill paying, automatic deposits and transfers, and accounts that exist purely online, with nothing physical to look at. It can be extremely difficult for someone taking over today, especially if they don't know passwords and usernames for web-based accounts.

That's why one of the things I do for clients is assemble what we call the Financial Inventory. We put together binders that include all of their necessary financial information. At the top is a letter to the beneficiaries that, if something happens to my clients, instructs the beneficiaries to call our office to help take care of everything. Whoever is involved will benefit from all of this information being together in one place.

Once you go from being a spouse to becoming single, there is a mountain of tasks to go through, such as what to do if your spouse is collecting Social Security and Medicare, how do you turn those payments off? And then, what happens if your spouse was getting a higher Social Security payment than you? All of that, on top of sifting through all the accounts and other details, gets much simpler if you're working with an advisor and have been involved in the planning conversations.

Providing Care

When a parent gets sick and needs assistance, it's hardly ever the son who's expected to handle that situation. It's the daughter who stops working to help with caregiving, which is completely unfair. It puts that woman in a bad financial spot, because now she is giving up some of her prime earning years at work.

This isn't just a hypothetical case. In fact, 61-percent of caregivers providing unpaid, informal care for the elderly are women. Furthermore, most of these women are still in the workforce.[34] In spite of that, women caregivers are losing close to $325,000 in wages and Social Security benefits as a result of shifting their time to being an unpaid caregiver.[35] This doesn't even count health care benefits and retirement savings. It also does not consider maternity care, mothers who homeschool, or women who leave the workforce to care for their children. Yikes, right?

Unofficial caregiving services in the U.S. are worth more than $150 billion—but that's still not the full cost. There's an emotional labor that women are providing that cannot be communicated through statistics alone. It can be exhausting work and emotionally taxing to watch a parent slowly decline. This can impact important relationships and the quality of the paid work you're still expected to produce.

The point of telling you this isn't to shock or scare you. I'm only trying to impart the significance of this work, as well as emphasize why it is so vital to prepare and plan for caregiving. Think about the caregivers, especially the women, who may be impacted, and how that financial and emotional burden can be lessened.

Parents never want to become a burden on their children, but a lot of parents are in denial that anything will ever happen to them. They think they'll never get to a point of needing caregiver services. That's why it can be imperative for the children to say to their parents, "Hey, let's take some time to look at your financial situation. Let's see if your resources will last. Let's look at whether you have any coverage from long-term care." And that can be the time to say, "Look, we would

---

[34] Anne-Marie Botek. AgingCare. April 19, 2022. "Sons vs. Daughters: The Role of Gender in Caring for Aging Parents."
https://www.agingcare.com/articles/daughters-care-more-for-parents-than-sons-171474.htm.

[35] Amy Barger and Christina Best. Caregiving.com. March 25, 2021. "The State of Women and Caregiving."
https://www.caregiving.com/posts/women-and-caregiving-2021.

love to take care of you, but that might not be an option at the time it comes about."

At the same time, women also need to know that, since they're the ones who tend to live longer and do it as a single person, they should also be looking ahead to what kind of care they might need as they age.

In general, women should probably be saving more money than their spouse, so if he's saving 5-percent or 10-percent in a 401(k) plan, she should be putting aside 12-percent or 15-percent. But, again, fortunately, women are better savers in general and better investors. So, when it comes to providing for their own future, women have a leg up on men, who tend to be more aggressive and reactionary when it comes to spending and investing.

Funding Your Own Retirement and Saving Money

We've mentioned that women tend to live longer than men, and they will face unique issues in their lifetimes. Therefore, it's vital that their retirements are well-funded! In addition to the traditional 401(k), there's also a spousal 401(k) that might be worth considering. This is where a spouse sets up an account on your behalf, and he or she can contribute part of their paycheck to help save for your retirement. When someone has dropped out of the workforce to care for a friend or relative, this can be a great option. Caregivers do have other options to remain in the workforce, though. They can talk to an employer's human resource department to see if there is paid leave, special circumstance, or sick leave options that may be available to them.

Some people, especially men, can make financial planning sound more complex and challenging than it really is, but there's absolutely no reason for any woman to feel intimidated about being involved in financial planning and controlling her own financial future. And the reason is very simple—women need more money to fund their retirements, period.

The good news is that women tend to be good at certain financial skills like saving, investing, and paying down debt – even better than men, on average. The more we encourage women to engage in their finances and the financial planning process, the better off EVERYONE will be!

CHAPTER 9
You Can't Take It with You

Unless you've got a map showing the location of the Fountain of Youth, your financial plan needs to include what happens to your money when you're gone. Tax issues are a huge factor here, but so are some simple things that often get overlooked—a will, a durable power of attorney, and a healthcare power of attorney. Without the basics, an estate can get tied up in probate court for years at a cost that eats up significant assets.

Establishing an Estate Plan

While everyone needs to have a basic estate plan, the more successful you are, the more important it is to have a plan put in place earlier than you might expect. People who have accumulated highly valuable assets or highly valued businesses, might even need to work around the Estate Tax, which is in flux every few years. Structuring assets in an estate the right way can be the key to avoiding the Estate Tax altogether.

In addition, a good estate plan means that your priorities are taken care of and that your remaining money goes where you want it to end up, whether that's to support children and grandchildren, benefit a charity, or help support your community.

The first part of any estate plan is a good, comprehensive—and up-to-date—will. A lot of people never get around to writing their wills, and that's understandable. It's complicated, it's technical, it can be expensive, and nobody wants to spend time and effort thinking about their own death. Another thing I commonly see is a family who went through all that trouble and contemplated their own mortality to create a will—but it's outdated. It may have been written before one or more of their children were born; it might include other relatives who have since died; it might even give all the assets to a now-ex-spouse. An old, outdated will is probably just as bad as having no will at all, because it means you could end up in probate court and whatever assets you wanted to pass on end up going to lawyers.

After a will, most people will need some kind of trust to pass assets on to their children, and the specific type and structure of the trust will change from person to person, depending on the family situation.

A larger, more comprehensive estate plan should be created when there are a lot of assets, such as a business, farm, real estate holdings, or other investments that total more than $11.4 million per person and would thus be subject to the federal estate tax. People like to joke that inheriting more than $11-million wouldn't be a problem, but if estate taxes apply, that money quickly gets cut by more than 40-percent.

If you're a parent of minor children, a trust can help establish who will care for your children in case of your untimely demise. It also establishes a structure for how the assets get used for your children's benefit; when the children can manage the assets for themselves; what happens to your home–will the children live there or move into someone else's home?; and many other factors.

If one or both individuals in a married couple have been previously married, having a trust can define whose children are entitled to which assets, and what to do with the proceeds of a house sale in this situation.

Furthermore, everyone should have a durable power of attorney, which gives a spouse or other trusted individual the ability to make decisions on the client's behalf should that client become incapacitated. They also need to have a health care power of attorney, which provides the same authority if the client is unable to make their own medical decisions.

Those are the basics. Even if you think you don't have any significant assets, you should take the time to get all of that covered if you don't want to leave your loved ones sorting out a gigantic legal mess after you're gone.

Make a Digital Copy

Maintaining a digital copy of your important documents is important long before you pass on.

What happens if you have a fire or flood?

In our online Client Portal, clients can log in and upload any kind of document to their Vault. I advise everyone to upload a copy of their most important documents there, such as their trust, their house deed, etc. I always say, you never know what might happen or when you might need access to these documents!

I know an advisor in California. A few years back, there were incredible wildfires in her community that literally burned down half the homes in her small town. Her clients were relieved when they realized that their most important documents were copied into their online Vault.

And it's not just wildfires—we've had a lot of floods here in Michigan, where documents can easily get destroyed. Prepare for the worst by protecting your important documents today.

The One-Hundred Year Plan

For most of my clients, we plan for both the spouses living until they're one hundred. If we plan for that lifespan, you're going to be fine in nearly all cases, but there are some circumstances that can be devastating. Relying on one spouse's pension or Social Security payment can put the surviving spouse in a terrible financial situation. Although the surviving spouse does get to keep the higher Social Security payment, that still can be a big cut in income for people. This is why I typically encourage people to elect a 100-percent survivorship on their pensions, if there's not too much of a reduction in benefit.

In most cases, it's best to take some sort of survivorship option if you're part of a married couple, even though it does reduce the initial pension payment for the retiree. Each company structures their pension differently, so a 50-percent, 65-percent, or 75-percent survivor option can be more advantageous, depending on the company. In Michigan, many of the automotive companies have a pension structure that makes the 65-percent survivor option the best option bar none. The key is to analyze all the available pension options, just like when considering a pension versus a lump sum. Generally, you will want some sort of survivor benefit on a pension to protect your spouse.

When we plan for two people to live until age one-hundred and one person passes away, the surviving spouse's expenses do go down a bit, but they certainly don't get cut in half. Think about fixed costs like a mortgage, utilities, or property taxes. Those expenses are the same whether there's one or two of you. That's why we plan for both spouses living a maximum lifespan, because whatever a couple is spending when they're ninety-two years old, is going to be pretty similar to the amount needed to support that household if one of them passes away.

Helping Survivors

It is very common that one person within a couple tends to handle the financial aspects of their lives, with the other spouse staying in the background on that topic. After the death of a spouse, we have to help clients adjust financially. I hear it all the time from new people coming to meet with me: "I handle all the money for our household. But if something happens to me, my spouse is going to need help. That is why I'm here today. I need to know that if I pass away first, my spouse has a trusted financial professional."

It has always been of utmost importance to me to help out a surviving spouse or the children of a client who passes away. To assist with this process, all of my clients get our Financial Binder. Not only does this house important financial documents and information, but the very first page speaks directly to the beneficiaries. It is a letter signed by the clients, instructing their beneficiaries to contact me and my firm if something happens. We are here to help, and we *want* to help. I have received phone calls from just-widowed spouses, saying that some of their loved one's last words were to call me. In a time of deep emotional distress, it comforts me to know that I can provide stability and guidance through a difficult time.

The longer I've worked in this industry, the more client deaths I must face. It is emotional to lose a long-time client. People don't always realize that advisors feel a real bond and connection with their clients. I suppose that's not the case for everyone, but it certainly is for me. There are a lot of emotions wrapped up in losing a client that I've built a relationship with over the years, but it helps to know that I can help the surviving spouse and kids.

It's not uncommon among financial advisors to have a surviving spouse come in with no idea what accounts the husband or wife had opened, what insurance policies were purchased, and so on. This does not have to happen. At my firm, we do several things for clients to help their survivors handle their final affairs.

First is the aforementioned Financial Binder that we give to all clients, which includes a listing of all of their financial accounts. Second, there is a Survivor's Checklist that lists all the important steps the children or surviving spouse should take in the first thirty, sixty, and ninety days after a death. This includes tasks like calling Social Security, calling utility companies, as well as meeting with us to do an amended financial plan based on this new reality. Third, we provide our clients access to an online Vault where they can keep any important documents. I call this our "online safety deposit box" where they can keep anything they feel would be valuable to their family after they pass. This Vault is only viewable to the client and whoever the client decides to share it with. My office staff and I don't have access to it, but access can be gained for a beneficiary once someone passes away.

Putting Affairs in Order

When we're dealing with a client's final affairs, there are three things that need to be handled.

The first is identifying all the accounts. This is pretty easy for beneficiaries of our clients because we provide an online financial dashboard. Not only does this dashboard show the accounts that our firm manages, but outside accounts can be linked, such as bank accounts, 401(k) accounts with current employers, etc. At any point, we can log into the dashboard and see exactly where all the assets are and how much they're worth.

The second task is to identify all of the beneficiaries on the accounts and ensure these are updated. The beneficiaries are the people designated on an account to receive those assets when you pass away, whether it's a bank account, an investment account, a 401(k) workplace plan, or an insurance policy.

Usually, you designate a beneficiary at the time of opening an account. Unfortunately, a lot of people never go back and reconsider or review those beneficiary designations. If someone passes away who hasn't planned things properly, it can get very messy and complicated. For example, all your assets could go to an ex-spouse or a deceased parent, which means you're going to end up in probate court for a judge to determine how your assets get distributed. This is a lengthy, expensive process that could have been avoided. Getting a list of all your beneficiaries is something we always encourage because it is critically important.

One issue that a lot of people don't understand is that there is a limited amount of time to take care of these affairs after someone passes away. Many people think they have five-years to take care of everything, but you don't. If IRA investments are involved, you really only have a year to decide how to structure that payout or you can face a big tax hit. Also, the year in which someone dies is the last tax year that the surviving spouse can file taxes with the "married filing jointly" status. After that, you're filing as an individual taxpayer, which changes all your deductible limits, withholding, tax brackets, and so on.

You want to have all this lined up and organized before you pass away. You want to avoid any potential for your estate going through probate court. And you don't need to have a lot of assets to have an estate, by the way. The estate tax limit is several million dollars for an individual and twice that for a couple, but an estate can be much smaller–your car, your condo, and what's in your bank and retirement accounts. If your estate goes to probate, there will be attorney fees, filing fees, and court charges that can easily eat up a chunk of the assets, plus it can take up to two-years to get everything settled.

The problem is that during that time, you can't get at the assets—at all. If you need to sell investments for tax harvesting, you can't do it. If the market goes up or down, you can't rebalance or move to other investments. You can't even take money out of the bank to pay your bills. In the case of simply maintaining a home, if somebody has passed away and the kids don't have the money to pay the taxes, maintenance, and other basics, it can be a huge issue.

It's absolutely necessary for the estate to have some liquidity, which is why there are the smaller final expense insurance policies, which provides immediate liquidity to the survivors. But, if you've done appropriate planning, that kind of coverage isn't necessary. That means you can avoid what used to be called "burial" insurance coverage, which is now marketed as "final expenses" insurance. These are unnecessary, expensive policies to provide money to handle funeral expenses, medical bills, etc., after someone dies. But anyone with a decent estate plan can skip these things.

When a spouse dies, for the most part, things are going to be complicated, even when you've been working with a planner. What's mostly involved is changing names on accounts and some basic financial housekeeping, and it doesn't need to be done right away. I always tell people, just take some time, we have a year. In fact, for some things, it's better to wait a couple of months when things are a little more settled.

The important thing to figure out at that point is what will the surviving spouse need now, and what's going to change in terms of his or her financial picture? Right after someone passes away, you really don't know what will change, whether their expenses have gone down or by how much, whether the surviving spouse needs money from the investments, and so on.

The Next Generation

After the surviving spouse dies and the assets are being passed on to their children or to others, then the process of planning starts all over again. In many cases, the kids haven't done much saving or planning on their own, so it's extra money that I hope they'll use for their retirement or other longer-term needs. In most cases, I try to emphasize that if they leave this money invested appropriately for their own situation, it can be a huge head start for their retirement and a wonderful legacy that their loved one has provided.

In many cases, surviving family members want to do something big, like, "We're taking everybody to Disney World!" And when I say everybody, I mean *everybody*. Kids, grandkids, nieces, nephews, aunts, and their long-lost third cousin. That sounds nice and very generous, but it's super expensive. I hate to see someone spend their whole inheritance on one fancy long weekend. I'm glad to say that in my professional experience, most people do the responsible thing and keep that money invested. They avoid considering it as a windfall. It gives their retirement savings a huge boost.

I really enjoy seeing that happen, because it means that, as an advisor, I've not only helped my original clients invest and preserve their assets and retire successfully, but I'm also helping the next generation set themselves up to follow the same paths. Beyond any money that's passed on, the real value of that kind of inheritance is that it builds even more financial security for others in the family for decades to come.

Acknowledgments

I would like to extend a huge *Thank You* to all the people who helped make this book a reality. To Brian, Erika, Jammie, and the AE Team, thank you for helping me get words on paper and stay on task. Thank you to my clients for inspiring me every day. To my parents, thank you for teaching me fiscal responsibility, and to my dad for leaving the legacy that allowed me to carve my own path. Thank you to my wife, Erika, and our three kids, Dylan, Elliana, and Mason, for your involvement, dedication, and sacrifices so I can continue helping others. And thank you to my Wealth Trac team; I couldn't do what I do without you.

KURT T. FILLMORE, CFF®

About the Author

**Kurt T. Fillmore, Founder & President,
Certified Financial Fiduciary®
Wealth Trac Financial**

As the founder and president of Wealth Trac Financial, LLC, Kurt Fillmore is focused on helping clients work toward their financial dreams through well-thought-out strategies for every stage of life.

The son of two teachers, Kurt was abruptly thrown into the finance world at nineteen-years-old when his father passed away unexpectedly. Unprepared to deal with this tragic loss, Kurt relied on his father's financial advisor to manage the money. Through tax mismanagement and poor investment choices, Kurt's inheritance was worth a fraction of its original value just a few years later.

At the time of his father's passing, Kurt was a student studying Finance at one of the top-ranked business schools in the nation, the Ross School of Business at the University of Michigan in Ann Arbor. He began educating himself on personal financial strategies and the details regarding his own situation. It was then that Kurt decided his goal in life: To use the knowledge he gained to help other families secure their futures and avoid large financial setbacks like he experienced at such a young age.

Following graduation, Kurt spent two years as an account executive at CitiGroup, where he managed retirement assets for medical professionals. He was named National Financial Counselor of the Year in 2002 and 2003.

Kurt became an independent advisor in 2004, ultimately founding Wealth Trac Financial in 2007. He is a Certified Financial Fiduciary®, holds his Series 65 securities license, and holds his life and health insurance license in many states across the USA. Kurt makes it his responsibility to thoroughly understand clients' goals and dreams and to leverage his knowledge and experience to help clients realize them.

Kurt has been featured on national and local news outlets for his industry knowledge, including Forbes, CNN, Consumer Reports, US News & World Report, Detroit FOX-2 News, and Kiplinger.

Kurt lives in the suburbs of Detroit, Michigan, with his wife, Erika, and three children, Dylan, Elliana, and Mason. In his free time, Kurt enjoys volunteering with Cub Scouts, attending musical events like concerts, the symphony, and the opera,